US Citizenship Test Study Guide 2023-2024

USCIS Naturalization Test Prep, Comprehensive Civics Practice with Q&A for Every Step.

By

Manuel Cordero

TABLE OF CONTENT

INTRODUCTION: THE AMERICAN DREAM

The allure of the American Dream has beckoned countless individuals from diverse backgrounds, ages, and nations. It's an ethos woven deeply into the fabric of the nation, representing a beacon of hope, opportunity, and liberty. At its core, the American Dream embodies the promise of a life full of possibilities, where one's endeavors, regardless of their origins, can lead to success, prosperity, and happiness in this vast land of opportunity.

Yet, beyond the shimmering horizon of this dream lies a crucial step for many: the path to American citizenship. Becoming a U.S. citizen is not merely a bureaucratic milestone. It's a profound transformation, a pledge of allegiance to a country's ideals, values, and its collective dream. By embarking on this journey, you're not just seeking legal status; you are embracing an identity, becoming part of a centuries-old tapestry that has been woven by millions who came before you, each adding their unique thread to the story of America.

Understanding the naturalization process, however, can sometimes feel overwhelming. The seemingly endless forms, the intricate legal jargon, the daunting interviews, and, of course, the civic and language tests can make the journey appear challenging. But this is where the purpose of this guide comes into focus. Designed with your success in mind, this book aims to simplify, clarify, and demystify the process, ensuring that the road to your American Dream is navigated with confidence and clarity.

This guide serves as your compass, providing a clear direction through the intricacies of the naturalization process. By its end, you will be equipped with the knowledge you need about application forms, procedures, and eligibility criteria. Beyond that, you'll find comprehensive coverage of the USCIS Civics questions, ensuring you not only know the answers but understand the deeper significance behind them. And as you prepare for your interview, this guide will be there, offering insights, tips, and real-life anecdotes to bolster your confidence.

Yet, beyond the facts, figures, and procedures, it's essential to remember the heart of this journey. Every step you take toward American citizenship is a step towards realizing your own version of the American Dream. Whether it's the promise of freedom, the pursuit of opportunity, or the simple desire to belong to a nation that values diversity and unity in equal measure, your dream is valid, valuable, and very much achievable.

In essence, this isn't just a guide to American citizenship; it's a guide to fulfilling your aspirations, to embracing a new identity, and to becoming an integral part of the ever-evolving story of America. Welcome to the journey towards your American Dream.

CHAPTER 2: UNDERSTANDING THE NATURALIZATION PROCESS

The path to American citizenship, though filled with steps and processes, is a journey paved with promise and purpose. Embarking on this voyage with clarity is not just about fulfilling the legal prerequisites, but also about understanding the spirit and ethos of the land one aspires to call home. This chapter breaks down the naturalization process, clears the fog around common misconceptions, and emphasizes the essence of preparedness.

1. THE NATURALIZATION OVERVIEW

Naturalization is the legal procedure that allows eligible foreign-born individuals to become U.S. citizens. At its core, the process ensures that aspirants are committed, informed, and resonate with American values. It begins with ensuring eligibility, moves through understanding and completing the requisite forms, and culminates in taking the Oath of Allegiance.

2. INITIAL ELIGIBILITY CHECK

Before one dive deep, it's crucial to understand whether they meet the basic eligibility criteria set by the USCIS. These criteria might include factors like age, duration of permanent residency, physical presence, moral character, and more. Ensuring that you align with these requirements is the first gate to pass.

Here's a comprehensive breakdown of these prerequisites:

a. Age Requirement:

Applicants must be at least 18 years old at the time of filing for naturalization. Minors have a different path through their U.S. citizen parents, either by derivation or acquisition.

b. Residency Status:

To apply for naturalization, an individual must have been a permanent resident (green card holder) of the U.S. for at least five years. For those married to U.S. citizens, this period is reduced to three years.

c. Continuous Residence:

Continuous residence means the applicant has made the U.S. their primary home. Temporary or short trips abroad won't disrupt this, but extended absences might. Generally, trips longer than six months can break continuous residence.

d. Physical Presence:

Over the last five years (or three years for spouses of U.S. citizens), the applicant should have been physically present in the U.S. for at least half the time.

e. State or District Residency:

Applicants must have lived in the state or USCIS district where they plan to apply for at least three months prior to the application.

f. Good Moral Character:

USCIS evaluates the character of applicants to ensure they uphold the values of the U.S. This assessment looks into an individual's criminal history, honesty during the application process, and other pertinent factors.

g. English and Civics Proficiency:

To be naturalized, one needs to display a basic understanding of U.S. history and government (civics) and demonstrate an ability to read, write, and speak basic English.

h. Attachment to Constitutional Principles:

Applicants must show an understanding and acceptance of the U.S. Constitution's principles, demonstrating a willingness to support and defend them.

i. Military Service Exceptions:

Certain individuals with U.S. military service may qualify for exceptions or variations to the typical eligibility criteria. It's crucial to explore this if it applies to you.

3. FORM N-400, APPLICATION FOR NATURALIZATION

Central to the journey is the completion and submission of Form N-400. This form serves as your official application and should be approached with precision. Here, you'll be providing personal details, your history, affiliations, and more. Every detail counts, and accuracy is paramount. Let's break down the nuances of this pivotal document:

a. Overview of the Form:

Form N-400 is a multi-part document. Each section is meticulously designed to gather details that determine if the applicant upholds the principles valued by the U.S. government and is a fit candidate for citizenship.

b. Personal and Biographical Details:

This section seeks information about your full name, any other names you might have used (like maiden names), birth details, and other personal identifiers. It's imperative to ensure consistency in the data you provide, especially if you've filed other immigration forms previously.

c. Residency and Travel History:

Here, you'll list down your residence history for the past five (or three, for those applying through marriage) years. Additionally, the form requires a breakdown of any trips taken outside the U.S. during this period, including durations and destinations.

d. Affiliations and Associations:

This segment probes into any affiliations or memberships you might have, especially those that might raise concerns about your alignment with American values. Being forthright and honest here is crucial, as USCIS will conduct thorough background checks.

e. Moral Character Assessment:

Through a series of questions, this part assesses the moral fiber of the applicant. Questions might delve into topics like criminal history, financial delinquencies, or any misrepresentation in previous immigration applications.

f. English and Civics Testing Preparation:

While this form doesn't test you, it does inquire if you've taken any classes or preparation courses for the English and civics tests, providing a gauge of your readiness.

g. Accommodations for Disabilities:

For applicants with disabilities, there are provisions to request accommodations during the naturalization interview and testing. This part ensures everyone has a fair chance at the process.

h. Application Fee and Waivers:

Form N-400 comes with an associated fee, which varies based on age and certain other factors. Some applicants might be eligible for fee waivers, and this section offers guidance on the same.

i. Supporting Documents:

To validate the information, you provide in the form, there's a list of supporting documents you'll need to attach. This might include copies of your green card, marital documents, or tax returns, among others.

j. Final Checklist and Submission:

Before submission, ensure that every section is complete, every question is answered truthfully, and all supporting documents are attached. Any oversights can lead to processing delays or even denials.

4. THE USCIS BIOMETRICS APPOINTMENT

After successfully submitting the N-400, applicants are summoned for a biometrics appointment. This step involves capturing fingerprints, photograph, and signature — primary for security checks and identity verification. Here's a detailed look into this vital phase:

a. Purpose of the Appointment:

The primary goal of the biometrics appointment is to ensure the safety and security of the United States by verifying the applicant's identity and performing criminal and security checks. This is an essential step in determining the applicant's eligibility for citizenship.

b. What to Expect:

Upon arriving at a USCIS Application Support Center (ASC), you'll be required to submit your photograph, fingerprints, and sometimes, an iris scan. The procedure is relatively straightforward and is typically completed within 30 minutes.

c. Notification and Scheduling:

After submitting your Form N-400, USCIS will send you a notice specifying the date, time, and location of your biometrics appointment. While rescheduling is possible if absolutely necessary, it's crucial to attend the scheduled appointment to avoid delays in your application process.

d. Documents to Bring:

Ensure you have the USCIS biometrics appointment notice and a valid photo ID, such as a driver's license, passport, or green card. These documents are vital for identity verification during the appointment.

e. Biometrics Fee:

There's a separate fee associated with the biometrics appointment, which covers the cost of collecting, processing, and storing your biometric data. This fee is usually paid when you submit your Form N-400, but it's wise to confirm payment details before the appointment.

f. What Happens Next?

Post your biometrics appointment, USCIS will utilize the collected data to run background checks against federal criminal and security databases. This ensures that the applicant hasn't been involved in activities that would make them ineligible for citizenship.

g. Potential Delays:

While the biometrics process is typically straightforward, issues such as unclear fingerprints might necessitate a second appointment. It's rare but essential to be prepared for such eventualities.

h. Security of Your Data:

USCIS takes the privacy and security of applicants' data seriously. The collected biometric information is stored securely and is accessible only to authorized personnel for official purposes.

i. Impact on the Naturalization Timeline:

The time taken to process the biometrics and subsequent background checks can influence the overall timeline of your naturalization journey. While most applicants receive an update or notice for their citizenship interview within a few months post the biometrics, it can vary based on individual cases and the volume of applications at the USCIS

5. PREPARING FOR THE USCIS INTERVIEW AND EXAMS

Perhaps the most anticipated step in the journey is the USCIS interview. Here, applicants not only showcase their knowledge about the U.S. but also their proficiency in the English language. Being prepared, practicing, and understanding potential questions can be a difference-maker. Adequate preparation is key to successfully navigating this stage, and here's what you need to know:

a. Purpose of the USCIS Interview:

The USCIS interview allows the immigration officer to verify the information provided in your application, assess your command of English, and administer the Civics test. It's also an opportunity for you to clarify any discrepancies in your application.

b. Notification of the Interview:

You'll receive a notice from USCIS that includes the date, time, and location of your interview. This notice typically arrives several weeks in advance, providing ample time for preparation.

c. Preparation for the Interview:

Begin with a thorough review of your N-400 application, especially focusing on the parts addressing moral character, as these can raise red flags if not properly addressed. Brush up on basic English communication skills, as you'll be assessed on your ability to understand, read, and write in English.

d. The Civics Test:

The civics test is a key part of the interview, designed to assess your knowledge of U.S. history and government. Of the 100 questions provided in the study materials, you will be asked up to 10, and you must answer correctly at least six to pass. Regular and systematic study using available USCIS materials can greatly improve your performance on this test.

e. On the Day of the Interview:

Arrive early, dress appropriately, and bring all requested documents, including your interview notice, green card, passports, and any other documents relevant to your case. Be prepared for the fact that the officer may ask questions about your background, application, and moral character.

f. Communicating Effectively During the Interview:

Listening carefully, answering honestly, and asking for clarifications if a question is unclear are all key to a successful interview. If you don't know the answer to a question, it's better to admit it than to guess incorrectly.

g. Potential Outcomes of the Interview:

At the end of the interview, the officer may approve your application, continue your case (if they need additional documents or if you failed the tests), or deny your application. In case of a denial, you'll receive a notice explaining the reasons and information about your rights to appeal.

h. What Happens Next:

If you pass the interview and tests, you'll eventually receive a notice to take the Oath of Allegiance, the final step in becoming a U.S. citizen. If your case is continued, follow the instructions provided by the officer to complete the requirements.

6. THE OATH OF ALLEGIANCE

The final, ceremonial step! Once the USCIS approves the naturalization application post-interview, applicants participate in a public ceremony. Here, they take the Oath of Allegiance, officially marking their transformation into American citizens. Here's a deeper dive into the significance, procedure, and emotions intertwined with this pivotal ceremony:

a. Understanding the Significance:

At its core, the Oath of Allegiance is a pledge of loyalty to the United States. By taking this oath, you're affirming your commitment to uphold the Constitution, defend the country, and renounce allegiances to other sovereigns. It's a solemn promise to be a dedicated, law-abiding citizen.

b. Receiving the Ceremony Invitation:

After successfully completing the USCIS interview and exams, you'll receive an official notification called the "Notice of Naturalization Oath Ceremony." This document provides essential details about the ceremony's date, time, and venue.

c. Preparation for the Ceremony:

While the oath ceremony is a celebratory event, there are still important administrative steps to address. Arrive early and bring the necessary documentation, especially the "Notice of Naturalization Oath Ceremony" and your Permanent Resident Card (Green Card). You'll be required to hand over your Green Card as it will no longer be valid after you become a U.S. citizen.

d. The Ceremony Proceedings:

The event usually begins with the gathering of candidates, followed by a welcome speech from USCIS officials. Thereafter, you and other applicants will collectively recite the Oath of Allegiance. Some ceremonies might feature guest speakers, video presentations, or musical performances to highlight the significance of U.S. citizenship.

e. Receiving the Certificate of Naturalization:

Post the Oath, you'll be presented with your Certificate of Naturalization. This document serves as official proof of your U.S. citizenship. It's essential to review the certificate for any errors in your personal details and report them immediately to USCIS officials if found.

f. Embracing the Emotional Experience:

For many, the oath ceremony is profoundly emotional. It signifies the culmination of a journey filled with hope, challenges, persistence, and, finally, belonging. It's common for new citizens and their families to be overwhelmed with a sense of accomplishment, pride, and gratitude.

g. Post-Ceremony Steps:

With your new status as a U.S. citizen, you can now apply for a U.S. passport, register to vote, and fully participate in the democratic processes of your new home. It's also a good time to explore and understand the rights, benefits, and responsibilities that come with American citizenship.

7. COMMON MISCONCEPTIONS

Many believe that marrying a U.S. citizen automatically grants them citizenship, or that just by serving in the U.S. military, citizenship is guaranteed. Such misconceptions can lead to complacency or missteps.

a. Only Perfect English Speakers Can Become Citizens:

While English proficiency is a requirement, perfection is not. The focus is on basic understanding, reading, and writing. The USCIS doesn't expect poetic eloquence, but functional fluency.

b. Naturalization Guarantees Permanent Citizenship:

Although becoming a U.S. citizen grants numerous privileges, one can still be denaturalized under rare circumstances, like committing fraud during the naturalization process.

c. Dual Citizenship is Prohibited:

The U.S. allows dual citizenship. However, during the U.S. naturalization oath, one pledges allegiance to the U.S. This doesn't necessarily negate other citizenships but highlights one's primary allegiance.

d. If I Fail the Test Once, I'll Never Become a Citizen:

Not true. Applicants who don't pass the test the first time will be given another opportunity. Preparation and understanding the material are key.

e. Children Born Abroad to U.S. Citizens are Not U.S. Citizens:

Children born overseas to U.S. citizens usually have a claim to U.S. citizenship, though there are stipulations and processes to follow to confirm this status.

f. Marriage to a U.S. Citizen Instantly Grants Citizenship:

Marrying a U.S. citizen may expedite the residency requirement, but the naturalization process still applies. It's a common misconception that marriage provides an instantaneous path to citizenship.

g. All Criminal Records Disqualify You:

While certain criminal records can pose a barrier to naturalization, not all crimes lead to automatic disqualification. It's essential to consult with immigration attorneys to understand the implications of one's personal history.

8. THE IMPORTANCE OF PREPARATION

As with any significant endeavor in life, preparation is key. From understanding the timeline, gathering essential documents, practicing for the interview to mentally preparing for each phase — being ready can transform the daunting into the doable.

CHAPTER 3: APPLICATION FORMS AND PROCEDURES

The path to U.S. citizenship is paved with forms, documents, and official procedures. To successfully navigate this route, it's imperative to have a clear understanding of the paperwork involved, and the processes they anchor. This chapter aims to provide a meticulous guide on the essential forms and procedures you'll encounter on your naturalization journey.

1. THE CORNERSTONE: FORM N-400, APPLICATION FOR NATURALIZATION

What it is: Form N-400 is the primary document you will need to start the naturalization process. It's essentially your formal request to the U.S. government to grant you citizenship.

Filling it out: Pay close attention to each section. Provide accurate and truthful information. Being thorough can save you from delays or denials further down the road.

Essential tips:

- Use black ink if filling out by hand.
- Ensure your answers are legible.
- Double-check dates, names, and addresses for accuracy.
- Attach additional sheets if you need more space, but always label them clearly.

2. SUBMISSION AND ASSOCIATED FEES

- **Where to submit:** The USCIS provides designated addresses based on your residential location and whether you're using the U.S. Postal Service or a courier service. Always consult the USCIS website for the most current addresses.

- **Fees**: As of the last update, the filing fee for Form N-400 is $725, which includes both the application charge and the biometric services fee. However, these costs can change, so always verify the current fee structure on the USCIS website.

- **Fee Waiver:** Some applicants might qualify for a fee waiver based on specific criteria, such as financial hardship. USCIS provides guidelines on who can qualify and how to apply for this waiver.

3. SUPPORTING DOCUMENTATION: AN ESSENTIAL CHECKLIST

When submitting your Form N-400, you'll need to include certain supporting documents. Here's a brief checklist:

- **Proof of Green Card** (Permanent Residency): Clear copies, front and back.
- **Proof of Residence:** Utility bills, leases, or other official documents showcasing your continuous residence.
- **Marital Status Documents:** If applicable, marriage certificates, divorce decrees, or death certificates.

- **Other Documents:** Depending on your specific situation, you might need additional documentation, such as criminal records, travel documents, or tax returns.

4. COMMON MISTAKES AND HOW TO SIDESTEP THEM

Navigating the maze of forms and documents can be tricky. Here are some common pitfalls:

- **Incomplete Forms:** This is perhaps the most frequent error. Ensure every field is filled out, even if the answer is "N/A" or "None."

- **Incorrect Fee Payment:** Double-check the amount, and always use the payment methods approved by USCIS.

- **Mismatched Information:** Ensure the details you provide match those on your supporting documents, especially names, dates, and addresses.

- **Forgetting Signatures:** An unsigned application is an invalid one. Always sign where required.

5. AFTER SUBMISSION: THE WAITING GAME AND BEING PROACTIVE

Once your application is in the system, it's crucial to:

- **Track your application:** USCIS provides a receipt number with which you can monitor your application's status online.

- **Respond promptly:** If USCIS requires additional information or documents, address their requests quickly to avoid delays.

- **Stay Updated:** Always inform USCIS if you change your address during the application process.

CHAPTER 4: ELIGIBILITY AND REQUIREMENTS

Embarking on the journey to U.S. citizenship is a significant step, replete with both dreams and challenges. It is essential to ensure that you are fully aware of the necessary qualifications and meet the specified criteria to make this transition as smooth as possible. This chapter provides a comprehensive overview of the eligibility requirements for naturalization, giving you the tools, you need to assess your qualifications and understand the benchmarks you must meet.

1. RESIDENCY CONDITIONS

For most individuals, obtaining permanent resident status (often referred to as having a 'Green Card') is the first significant step on the road to citizenship. Once you are a permanent resident, a set period of residency within the United States is required before applying for citizenship.

- **Continuous Residency**: Typically, you must have been a permanent resident of the U.S. for at least five years. However, if you are married to a U.S. citizen, this duration is shortened to three years. Continuous residency means that you must not have taken any trips outside the U.S. that lasted six months or longer without proper documentation showing you did not abandon your resident status.

- **Physical Presence:** Over the last five years, you should have been physically present in the U.S. for at least half the time, which translates to 30 months. For those qualifying through marriage to a U.S. citizen, you should be physically present for at least 18 months out of the three years.

2. GOOD MORAL CHARACTER

The concept of 'Good Moral Character' is central to U.S. immigration policy. While it might sound subjective, the USCIS defines this in concrete terms:

- **No Serious Criminal Record:** Certain crimes, like murder or any sort of terrorism-related activities, permanently bar one from establishing good moral character. Other offenses, such as fraud, may make you ineligible if they occurred within the statutory period (typically five years before the application).

- **Honesty in Dealings:** This applies especially to your interactions with USCIS. Any dishonesty during the application process, even if it involves minor details, can be grounds for denial.

- **Fulfillment of Financial Obligations:** This includes paying taxes and providing child support, where applicable. Failure to uphold these responsibilities may be seen as evidence of bad moral character.

3. UNDERSTANDING AND SPEAKING BASIC ENGLISH

Language is a bridge to understanding culture, people, and the very ethos of a nation. Applicants must demonstrate:

- **Ability to Read, Write, and Speak:** Simple words and phrases in English are part of the test. Exceptions are made for certain age groups and long-term residents.

- **Basic Understanding of U.S. Government and History:** This is covered in detail in the USCIS Civics test, a pivotal component of the naturalization process.

4. ATTACHMENT TO THE U.S. CONSTITUTION

Believing in the principles of the U.S. Constitution and favorably disposing oneself to the good order and happiness of the U.S. is integral. This essentially means:

- **Support for Democratic Principles:** The U.S. stands as a beacon of democracy, and its citizens are expected to uphold and respect these principles.

- **Willingness to Serve:** This might include serving in the U.S. armed forces or performing civilian service for the U.S. when required by law.

CHAPTER 5: DECODING THE FINANCIAL ASPECTS

Embarking on the journey to U.S. citizenship is not just a commitment of time and effort; it also requires a financial commitment. Just like any major life event, whether it's purchasing a home, planning a wedding, or getting a college education, becoming a U.S. citizen comes with its associated costs. This chapter will serve as your guide through the financial maze of the naturalization process, ensuring that you are well-prepared to make this dream a reality without unexpected setbacks.

1. NATURALIZATION APPLICATION FEES

- **USCIS Application Fee for Form N-400:** This is the primary fee associated with the naturalization process. The cost covers the processing of your application, and it's important to stay updated on the exact amount as it can change.

- **Biometric Services Fee:** Alongside the application, the United States Citizenship and Immigration Services (USCIS) also requires some applicants to pay for biometric services, which covers fingerprinting and photographing.

It's crucial to note that fees can be updated periodically by the USCIS. Therefore, before submitting any payment, always refer to the USCIS website or contact their service center to confirm the current amounts.

2. FEE WAIVERS AND REDUCTIONS

- **Full Waivers:** Some applicants might qualify for a fee waiver, which means they won't need to pay the USCIS application or biometric fees. This is typically based on certain financial hardship criteria.

- **Fee Reduction:** In some instances, if an applicant doesn't qualify for a full waiver, they might still be eligible for a fee reduction based on their income.

Eligibility for both fee waivers and reductions is primarily determined by your current financial situation, such as being on a means-tested benefit, or having a household income below a specific percentage of the Federal Poverty Guidelines.

3. METHODS OF PAYMENT

- **Check or Money Order:** This should be made payable to the U.S. Department of Homeland Security. It's crucial not to abbreviate the name.

- **Credit Card:** USCIS accepts credit card payments for the N-400 application fee. If you choose this option, you'll need to submit Form G-1450, Authorization for Credit Card Transactions.

Avoid sending cash. If any issues arise with your payment – for instance, if a check bounces – it could delay your application or even lead to its rejection.

4. FINANCIAL PREPAREDNESS FOR THE NATURALIZATION JOURNEY

Navigating the path to citizenship requires not just understanding the associated fees but also planning for incidental costs.

- **Additional Documentation:** Sometimes, you might need to obtain certain records or documents that come with their own fees.

- **Travel Expenses:** Depending on your location, you might have to factor in travel costs to the nearest USCIS office for interviews or biometric appointments.

- **English and Civics Classes:** For those who feel they need additional preparation for the citizenship tests, enrolling in classes can be an extra expense.

5. COMMON FINANCIAL PITFALLS TO AVOID

- **Late or Missing Payments:** Ensure that you pay the required fees when submitting your application. Delayed or missing payments can lead to processing setbacks.

- **Overlooking Possible Waivers:** Before submitting your payment, thoroughly check if you're eligible for any waivers or reductions. Every dollar saved can be beneficial in your journey.

- **Incomplete Forms**: If using a credit card, ensure that Form G-1450 is filled out completely and correctly. An error can lead to processing delays.

CHAPTER 6: Q&A -MASTERING THE 100 USCIS CIVICS QUESTIONS

To many, the heart of the naturalization process is the Civics Test. These questions, encompassing a century-spanning narrative, encapsulate the ethos of the United States — its inception, development, governance, and societal values. Becoming a citizen is not just about living in a country but understanding its past, present, and the aspirations for its future. Through the 100 civics questions, one gets a taste of the rich tapestry that is America.

A. FOUNDATIONS OF AMERICAN DEMOCRACY

1. What is an amendment?

Answer: A change (to the Constitution) or an addition (to the Constitution).

Explanation: An amendment modifies the U.S. Constitution, either by refining existing provisions or introducing new ones. The Constitution has been amended 27 times, reflecting the nation's evolving values and needs.

2. What do we call the first ten amendments to the Constitution?

Answer: The Bill of Rights.

Explanation: Adopted shortly after the Constitution itself, the Bill of Rights safeguards essential individual liberties, such as freedom of speech, religion, and the press, from government interference.

3. What is one right or freedom from the First Amendment?

Answer: Speech (Other possible answers include religion, assembly, press, and the right to petition the government).

Explanation: The First Amendment is foundational, protecting multiple freedoms that are crucial for a functioning democracy. This ensures citizens can express and assemble freely, practice their religion, have a free press, and petition the government without fear of retribution.

4. How many amendments does the Constitution have?

Answer: Twenty-seven (27).

Explanation: While the Constitution has been amended 27 times since its adoption, the process to do so is rigorous, requiring significant consensus, which underscores the gravity and deliberation with which the nation evolves its foundational laws.

5. What did the Declaration of Independence do?

Answer: Announced our independence (from Great Britain), declared our independence (from Great Britain), said that the United States is free (from Great Britain).

Explanation: Drafted primarily by Thomas Jefferson and adopted on July 4, 1776, the Declaration of Independence formally proclaimed the thirteen American colonies' separation from British rule, outlining their grievances and their philosophy on human rights and governance.

6. What are two rights in the Declaration of Independence?

Answer: Life, Liberty, and the pursuit of Happiness.

Explanation: Derived from Enlightenment thinking, especially the philosophies of John Locke, these unalienable rights are foundational to American values, emphasizing that government's role is to protect these inherent human rights.

7. Freedom of religion means you can practice any religion, or not practice a religion.

Answer: True.

Explanation: One of the cornerstones of the American ethos is the freedom of belief. This ensures that every individual can freely choose and practice any religion or abstain from religious practices altogether without facing discrimination or persecution.

8. What is the economic system in the United States?

Answer: Capitalist economy.

Explanation: The United States operates on a capitalist economy, which emphasizes private ownership and the free market. In a capitalist system, decisions about production, investment, and distribution are driven by individuals or corporations in the marketplace, and prices for goods and services are determined by competition and consumer demand.

9. What is the rule of law?

Answer: Everyone must follow the law; leaders must obey the law; the government must obey the law; no one is above the law.

Explanation: The rule of law is a foundational principle in American democracy. It ensures that all entities, including the government and its officials, are subject to and accountable under the same laws. This principle is essential to maintain fairness, justice, and equality in society.

10. Name one branch or part of the government.

Answer: Congress (Other possible answers include the Presidency and the Judiciary).

Explanation: The U.S. government is structured with a system of checks and balances and is divided into three branches: the Legislative (Congress), the Executive (the President), and the Judicial (the Courts). This division ensures that power is not centralized and each branch can keep the others in check.

11. What stops one branch of government from becoming too powerful?

Answer: Checks and balances.

Explanation: The framers of the Constitution implemented the system of checks and balances to prevent any single branch of government from gaining unchecked power. This system allows each branch to challenge or "check" the powers of the other branches, ensuring a balance of power in the federal government.

12. Who is in charge of the executive branch?

Answer: The President.

Explanation: The President is the head of the executive branch of the U.S. government, responsible for implementing and enforcing federal laws. This branch also includes the Vice President and the President's Cabinet, which consists of the principal heads of the various executive departments.

13. Who makes federal laws?

Answer: Congress.

Explanation: Congress, comprising the Senate and the House of Representatives, is the legislative branch of the U.S. government responsible for creating federal laws. While the President has the power to veto a law, Congress can override this veto with a sufficient majority.

14. What are the two parts of the U.S. Congress?

Answer: The Senate and the House of Representatives.

Explanation: The U.S. Congress is bicameral, meaning it has two separate chambers: the Senate and the House of Representatives. The Senate represents each state equally, with two Senators from each state, while the House of Representatives is based on state population, with more populous states having more representatives.

15. How many U.S. Senators are there?

Answer: 100.

Explanation: The Senate is composed of two Senators from each of the 50 states, totaling 100 Senators. Each Senator serves a six-year term.

16. We elect a U.S. Senator for how many years?

Answer: Six years.

Explanation: U.S. Senators are elected to serve six-year terms. Senate elections are staggered, meaning that approximately one-third of the Senate is up for reelection every two years.

17. Who is one of your state's U.S. Senators now?

Answer: Answers will vary depending on the state.

Explanation: Each state has two U.S. Senators representing it in Congress. The specific Senators will depend on the state in question and the time of inquiry, as Senators may change due to elections, appointments, or other reasons.

18. The House of Representatives has how many voting members?

Answer: 435.

Explanation: The House of Representatives is composed of 435 voting members. The number of representatives each state has is based on its population, determined by the U.S. Census, which is conducted every 10 years.

19. We elect a U.S. Representative for how many years?

Answer: Two years.

Explanation: U.S. Representatives, or Congresspeople, are elected to serve two-year terms. All members of the House of Representatives face election or reelection every two years.

20. Name your U.S. Representative.

Answer: Answers will vary.

Explanation: The specific U.S. Representative for an individual will depend on the congressional district in which they reside. Each state has multiple districts, except for states with small populations, which may have just one representative for the entire state.

21. Who does a U.S. Senator represent?

Answer: All the people of the state.

Explanation: While U.S. Representatives serve constituents from a specific district within a state, U.S. Senators represent all residents and interests of their entire state.

22. Why do some states have more Representatives than other states?

Answer: Because of the state's population.

Explanation: The number of U.S. Representatives a state has is determined by its population. Every 10 years, the U.S. Census counts the population, and based on these numbers, states may gain or lose representatives. States with larger populations have more representatives than states with smaller populations.

23. We elect a President for how many years?

Answer: Four years.

Explanation: The President of the United States is elected to serve a four-year term. A President can be re-elected for one additional term, serving a maximum of eight years in total.

24. In what month do we vote for President?

Answer: November.

Explanation: Presidential elections are held every four years on the first Tuesday of November.

25. What is the name of the President of the United States now?

Answer: Answers will vary based on the current year and who is in office at the time.

Explanation: The President can change due to elections, impeachments, or other reasons. It's essential to refer to the current year to identify the sitting President.

26. What is the name of the Vice President of the United States now?

Answer: Answers will vary based on the current year and who is in office at the time.

Explanation: Like the President, the Vice President can change due to elections or other reasons. Checking the current administration will give the name of the current Vice President.

27. If the President can no longer serve, who becomes President?

Answer: The Vice President.

Explanation: In the line of succession, the Vice President is next in line to assume the Presidency if the sitting President can no longer fulfill their duties. This has been the protocol since the inception of the U.S. Constitution.

28. If both the President and the Vice President can no longer serve, who becomes President?

Answer: The Speaker of the House.

Explanation: If both the President and the Vice President are unable to serve, the Speaker of the House is next in the line of succession to assume the Presidency.

29. Who is the Commander in Chief of the military?

Answer: The President.

Explanation: The U.S. Constitution grants the President the role of Commander in Chief, giving them authority over the country's armed forces. This means the President has control over military operations and can make important decisions regarding national defense.

30. Who signs bills to become laws?

Answer: The President.

Explanation: Once Congress passes a bill, it goes to the President. If the President signs the bill, it becomes law. If the President vetoes or rejects it, Congress can still override the veto with a two-thirds majority vote in both the House and Senate.

31. Who vetoes bills?

Answer: The President.

Explanation: The President has the authority to veto or reject bills sent by Congress. A vetoed bill can still become a law if both houses of Congress vote to override the veto with a two-thirds majority.

32. What does the President's Cabinet do?

Answer: Advises the President.

Explanation: The President's Cabinet is composed of the heads of executive departments. They play a crucial role in the U.S. government, providing expertise and advice to the President on various national and international issues.

33. What are two Cabinet-level positions?

Answer: Answers may vary but could include positions like Secretary of State and Secretary of Defense.

Explanation: The President's Cabinet includes the heads of 15 executive departments like the Department of State, Department of Defense, Department of Education, etc. Each of these positions is vital in advising the President and overseeing their respective departments.

34. What does the judicial branch do?

Answer: Reviews laws, explains laws, resolves disputes (disagreements), decides if a law goes against the Constitution.

Explanation: The judicial branch, mainly consisting of courts, interprets the law, ensures justice, and checks if laws align with the U.S. Constitution. It acts as a counterbalance to the legislative and executive branches.

35. What is the highest court in the United States?

Answer: The Supreme Court.

Explanation: The Supreme Court, located in Washington, D.C., is the final arbiter in the federal judicial system. It handles cases that have significant implications for the Constitution and federal law.

36. How many justices are on the Supreme Court?

Answer: Nine.

Explanation: The Supreme Court is comprised of nine justices: one Chief Justice and eight Associate Justices.

37. Who is the Chief Justice of the United States now?

Answer: Answers will vary based on the current year and who is in office at the time.

Explanation: The Chief Justice is the head of the U.S. Supreme Court and holds the highest judicial position in the country. It's essential to refer to the current year to identify the sitting Chief Justice.

38. Under our Constitution, some powers belong to the federal government. What is one power of the federal government?

Answer: To print money.

Explanation: The U.S. Constitution grants specific powers to the federal government, like the power to coin and print money, declare war, establish post offices, and regulate commerce with foreign nations.

39. Under our Constitution, some powers belong to the states. What is one power of the states?

Answer: Provide schooling and education.

Explanation: Each state in the U.S. retains certain powers independent of the federal government. These include powers related to establishing and maintaining schools, conducting local elections, and regulating commerce within the state.

40. Who is the Governor of your state now?

Answer: Answers will vary based on the state and the current year.

Explanation: The Governor is the chief executive officer of a state and its responsibilities and powers vary among states. It's essential to check current information based on the state in question.

41. What is the capital of your state?

Answer: Answers will vary based on the state.

Explanation: Each of the 50 U.S. states has its own capital where the state government resides. For instance, the capital of California is Sacramento, while that of New York is Albany.

42. What are the two major political parties in the United States?

Answer: Democratic and Republican.

Explanation: Historically, the United States has been dominated by a two-party system, with the Democratic and Republican parties being the most influential in shaping the nation's politics.

43. What is the political party of the President now?

Answer: Answers will vary based on the current year and who is in office at the time.

Explanation: The President can belong to any political party, but historically, U.S. Presidents have predominantly been either Democratic or Republican.

44. What is the name of the Speaker of the House of Representatives now?

Answer: Answers will vary based on the current year and who is in office at the time.

Explanation: The Speaker of the House is the presiding officer of the U.S. House of Representatives. This position is filled through an election by the House's members, and the Speaker's party typically has a majority in the House.

B: SYSTEM OF GOVERNMENT
----

45. There are four amendments to the Constitution about who can vote. Describe one of them.

Answer: Citizens eighteen (18) and older can vote.

Explanation: Several amendments to the U.S. Constitution have expanded voting rights. The 26th Amendment, for example, lowered the voting age to 18, ensuring that younger citizens have a voice in elections.

46. What is one responsibility that is only for United States citizens?

Answer: Serve on a jury.

Explanation: While both U.S. citizens and permanent residents have many similar responsibilities, certain duties, such as serving on a jury, are exclusive to U.S. citizens.

47. What are two rights only for United States citizens?

Answer: Vote in a federal election and run for federal office.

Explanation: U.S. citizens have certain exclusive rights, including the right to vote in federal elections and the opportunity to run for federal public offices, such as the U.S. Senate or the House of Representatives.

48. What are two rights of everyone living in the United States?

Answer: Freedom of expression and freedom of worship.

Explanation: The U.S. Constitution and its amendments ensure certain fundamental rights to everyone residing in the country, regardless of their citizenship status. This includes the right to express oneself freely and the right to practice or abstain from any religion.

49. What do we show loyalty to when we say the Pledge of Allegiance?

Answer: The United States.

Explanation: The Pledge of Allegiance is a solemn oath expressing loyalty and devotion to the United States and its flag. Reciting the Pledge is a traditional practice in schools and various events, emphasizing unity and shared values.

50. What is one promise you make when you become a United States citizen?

Answer: Give up loyalty to other countries.

Explanation: When individuals are naturalized as U.S. citizens, they take an oath of allegiance to the United States, which signifies their commitment to this country and the renunciation of any prior allegiances.

51. How old do citizens have to be to vote for President?

Answer: Eighteen (18) and older.

Explanation: The 26th Amendment to the U.S. Constitution, ratified in 1971, granted the right to vote to all citizens aged 18 or older, acknowledging their maturity and capability to participate in the democratic process.

52. What are two ways that Americans can participate in their democracy?

Answer: Vote and join a political party.

Explanation: Active participation in a democratic society can take many forms. Voting in elections is a direct way to influence governmental decisions. Additionally, joining a political party allows individuals to support ideologies and policies they believe in.

53. When is the last day you can send in federal income tax forms?

Answer: April 15.

Explanation: April 15th is traditionally the deadline for filing federal income tax returns. If the date falls on a weekend or holiday, the deadline might be extended to the next business day.

54. When must all men register for the Selective Service?

Answer: At age eighteen (18).

Explanation: The Selective Service System requires that all male U.S. citizens and male immigrants, whether documented or undocumented, register within 30 days of their 18th birthday. This registration is crucial in case a military draft becomes necessary.

C: AMERICAN HISTORY -RIGHTS AND RESPONSABILITIES

55. What is one reason colonists came to America?

Answer: Freedom.

Explanation: Numerous colonists came to America seeking freedom, whether it was religious freedom, like the Pilgrims and Puritans, or the freedom to seek better economic opportunities.

56. Who lived in America before the Europeans arrived?

Answer: Native Americans.

Explanation: Long before European explorers set foot on the continent, diverse groups of Native Americans had established intricate cultures, societies, and civilizations across North America.

57. What group of people was taken to America and sold as slaves?

Answer: Africans.

Explanation: From the late 16th century to the 19th century, millions of African people were forcibly taken from their homes, transported across the Atlantic Ocean, and sold as slaves in the Americas.

58. Why did the colonists fight the British?

Answer: Because of high taxes (taxation without representation).

Explanation: Among various reasons, a primary grievance of the American colonists was the imposition of high taxes by the British without any representation in the British Parliament, leading to the popular cry, "No taxation without representation!"

59. Who wrote the Declaration of Independence?

Answer: Thomas Jefferson.

Explanation: While the drafting committee for the Declaration of Independence consisted of five members, including Benjamin Franklin and John Adams, it was Thomas Jefferson who was the principal author, penning the document's powerful and enduring words.

60. When was the Declaration of Independence adopted?

Answer: July 4, 1776.

Explanation: This date is celebrated annually as Independence Day in the U.S., marking the formal adoption of the Declaration by the Continental Congress and the announcement of the thirteen American colonies' decision to break away from British rule.

61. There were 13 original states. Name three.

Answer: New York, Virginia, and Massachusetts.

Explanation: The thirteen original states correspond to the thirteen colonies that declared independence from Britain. Other original states include New Hampshire, Maryland, Connecticut, Rhode Island, Delaware, North Carolina, South Carolina, Georgia, Pennsylvania, and New Jersey.

62. What happened at the Constitutional Convention?

Answer: The Constitution was written.

Explanation: In 1787, delegates from the various states convened in Philadelphia with the initial aim to amend the Articles of Confederation. However, they ended up drafting a new document, the U.S. Constitution, which laid the groundwork for the current structure and functions of the U.S. government.

63. When was the Constitution written?

Answer: 1787.

Explanation: The U.S. Constitution was drafted during the Constitutional Convention, which took place from May to September of 1787 in Philadelphia.

64. The Federalist Papers supported the passage of the U.S. Constitution. Name one of the writers.

Answer: James Madison.

Explanation: The Federalist Papers were a series of essays advocating for the ratification of the U.S. Constitution. Three key figures authored these essays under the pseudonym "Publius": James Madison, Alexander Hamilton, and John Jay.

65. What is one thing Benjamin Franklin is famous for?

Answer: U.S. diplomat.

Explanation: Benjamin Franklin wore many hats during his lifetime—writer, scientist, inventor, and statesman. One of his significant roles was as a diplomat, where he played a pivotal role in securing French support during the American Revolution.

66. Who is the "Father of Our Country"?

Answer: George Washington.

Explanation: George Washington, the first President of the United States, is often referred to as the "Father of Our Country" because of the pivotal leadership role he played in the founding of the nation, both during the Revolutionary War and as the inaugural president.

67. Who was the first President?

Answer: George Washington.

Explanation: After the U.S. Constitution was ratified, George Washington was unanimously elected as the first President of the United States, serving two terms from 1789 to 1797.

68. What territory did the United States buy from France in 1803?

Answer: Louisiana.

Explanation: The United States acquired a vast area of land from France in 1803 through the Louisiana Purchase. This acquisition, made during President Thomas Jefferson's administration, doubled the size of the United States and provided territory for westward expansion.

69. Name one war fought by the United States in the 1800s.

Answer: The Civil War.

Explanation: The U.S. Civil War, fought from 1861 to 1865, was a major conflict between the Northern states (Union) and the Southern states (Confederacy) primarily over issues of slavery and states' rights. Other wars during the 1800s include the War of 1812, the Mexican-American War, and the Spanish-American War.

70. Name the U.S. war between the North and the South.

Answer: The Civil War.

Explanation: The Civil War, which lasted from 1861 to 1865, was a defining moment in U.S. history. It was fought over the preservation of the Union and the question of whether slavery would continue in the Southern states.

71. Name one problem that led to the Civil War.

Answer: Slavery.

Explanation: The issue of slavery was central to the tensions between the Northern and Southern states. The North generally sought to limit the expansion of slavery, while the South defended the institution as vital to its economy and way of life.

72. What was one important thing that Abraham Lincoln did?

Answer: Freed the slaves (Emancipation Proclamation).

Explanation: President Abraham Lincoln issued the Emancipation Proclamation on January 1, 1863, which declared that all slaves in Confederate-held territory were to be set free. This was a crucial step in the abolition of slavery in the United States.

73. What did the Emancipation Proclamation do?

Answer: Freed the slaves in the Confederate states.

Explanation: While the Emancipation Proclamation did not immediately free all slaves, it declared that slaves in territories rebelling against the Union were to be freed. This shifted the character of the Civil War, linking it directly with the cause of abolition.

74. What did Susan B. Anthony do?

Answer: Fought for women's rights.

Explanation: Susan B. Anthony was a pioneering advocate for women's suffrage in the United States. She played a key role in the women's rights movement, working diligently to secure the right to vote for women, a goal realized with the passage of the 19th Amendment in 1920.

75. Name one war fought by the United States in the 1900s.

Answer: World War I.

Explanation: World War I, also known as the Great War, lasted from 1914 to 1918, although the U.S. joined in 1917. It involved many of the world's great powers, including the U.S., and reshaped the political map of the world. Other wars in the 1900s include World War II, the Korean War, the Vietnam War, and the Gulf War.

76. Who was President during World War I?

Answer: Woodrow Wilson.

Explanation: Woodrow Wilson served as the 28th President of the United States from 1913 to 1921, and he led the nation during its involvement in World War I. Wilson later played a key role in the post-war peace conference and the drafting of the League of Nations, though the U.S. never joined.

77. Who was President during the Great Depression and World War II?

Answer: Franklin Roosevelt.

Explanation: Franklin D. Roosevelt, often referred to as FDR, was the 32nd President of the United States. He served four terms from 1933 to 1945 and led the country through some of its most challenging times, including the Great Depression and the majority of World War II.

78. Who did the United States fight in World War II?

Answer: Japan, Germany, and Italy.

Explanation: During World War II, the main adversaries of the U.S. were the Axis Powers, which consisted of Japan, Germany, and Italy. The conflict spanned various theaters of war, including Europe and the Pacific.

79. Before he was President, Eisenhower was a general. What war was he in?

Answer: World War II.

Explanation: Dwight D. Eisenhower served as a general during World War II and played a pivotal role in the planning and execution of the D-Day invasion in 1944. He later became the 34th President of the United States.

80. During the Cold War, what was the main concern of the United States?

Answer: Communism.

Explanation: The Cold War, spanning from the end of World War II to the early 1990s, was characterized by political, military, and economic tensions between the Western bloc (led by the U.S.) and the Eastern bloc (led by the Soviet Union). The main concern for the U.S. during this period was the spread of communism.

81. What movement tried to end racial discrimination?

Answer: Civil Rights Movement.

Explanation: The Civil Rights Movement, which took place primarily during the 1950s and 1960s, sought to end racial segregation and discrimination against African Americans. It led to landmark legislation like the Civil Rights Act of 1964 and the Voting Rights Act of 1965.

82. What did Martin Luther King, Jr. do?

Answer: Fought for civil rights and equality for all Americans.

Explanation: Dr. Martin Luther King, Jr. was a pivotal figure in the Civil Rights Movement. He advocated for nonviolent resistance and played a key role in significant events such as the Montgomery Bus Boycott, the March on Washington, and the Selma to Montgomery marches. His famous "I Have a Dream" speech is emblematic of his mission for a nation where individuals are judged by their character, not the color of their skin.

83. What major event happened on September 11, 2001, in the United States?

Answer: Terrorists attacked the United States.

Explanation: On September 11, 2001, 19 militants associated with the extremist group al-Qaeda hijacked four airplanes. Two of the planes were flown into the Twin Towers of the World Trade Center in New York City, causing the towers to collapse. Another plane hit the Pentagon, and the fourth plane, United Airlines Flight 93, crashed in Pennsylvania after passengers attempted to overcome the hijackers.

84. Name one American Indian tribe in the United States.

Answer: Navajo (Note: There are many correct answers, including but not limited to Cherokee, Sioux, Chippewa, Choctaw, Apache, Iroquois, Creek, Blackfeet, Seminole, Cheyenne, etc.)

Explanation: Native American tribes have diverse histories and cultures. The Navajo, for instance, are known for their significant contribution during World War II as the Navajo Code Talkers, who used their native language to transmit coded messages.

D: SYMBOLS AND HOLIDAYS

85. Name one of the two longest rivers in the United States.

Answer: Missouri River (The other correct answer is the Mississippi River.)

Explanation: The Missouri River is the longest river in the U.S., spanning over 2,300 miles. It merges with the Mississippi River, which is the second-longest, and together they form the fourth largest river system in the world.

86. What ocean is on the West Coast of the United States?

Answer: Pacific Ocean.

Explanation: The Pacific Ocean is the largest and deepest ocean in the world and spans the entire western coastline of the United States.

87. What Ocean is on the East Coast of the United States?

Answer: Atlantic Ocean.

Explanation: The Atlantic Ocean is the second-largest ocean in the world. It borders the eastern U.S. coastline and extends from the Arctic in the north to the Antarctic in the south.

88. Name one U.S. territory.

Answer: Puerto Rico (Other correct answers include Guam, the U.S. Virgin Islands, American Samoa, the Northern Mariana Islands, etc.)

Explanation: U.S. territories are regions that are neither a U.S. state nor an independent country. Puerto Rico, for example, is an island located in the Caribbean, and its residents are U.S. citizens.

89. Name one state that borders Canada.

Answer: New York (Other correct answers include Alaska, Idaho, Maine, Michigan, Minnesota, Montana, New Hampshire, North Dakota, Vermont, and Washington.)

Explanation: Several U.S. states share a border with Canada, our neighbor to the north. For example, New York shares an extensive boundary with the Canadian provinces of Ontario and Quebec, including both land borders and the watery expanse of the Great Lakes.

90. Name one state that borders Mexico.

Answer: Texas (Other correct answers include California, Arizona, and New Mexico.)

Explanation: The United States shares a southern border with Mexico. Texas has the longest stretch of this border, encompassing various terrains from major urban areas to the Rio Grande's winding river path.

91. What is the capital of the United States?

Answer: Washington, D.C.

Explanation: Washington, D.C., formally known as the District of Columbia, serves as the capital of the United States. Unlike other cities, it does not belong to any state. The land was designated as the nation's capital in the late 18th century and was selected to be on the Potomac River between the states of Maryland and Virginia.

92. Where is the Statue of Liberty?

Answer: New York Harbor (Liberty Island)

Explanation: The Statue of Liberty, a gift from the people of France to the United States, stands as a symbol of freedom and democracy. While it's situated on Liberty Island in New York Harbor, it can be seen from various points in New York City, especially from Battery Park.

93. Why does the flag have 13 stripes?

Answer: Because there were 13 original colonies.

Explanation: The 13 stripes on the U.S. flag represent the 13 original colonies that declared independence from Britain in 1776. These colonies became the first states of the United States.

94. Why does the flag have 50 stars?

Answer: Because there are 50 states.

Explanation: Each star on the flag represents a U.S. state. Since there are 50 states in the U.S., there are 50 stars on the flag.

95. What is the name of the national anthem?

Answer: The Star-Spangled Banner.

Explanation: "The Star-Spangled Banner" was written by Francis Scott Key during the War of 1812 after witnessing the bombardment of Fort McHenry and seeing the American flag still flying the next morning. It became the official national anthem in 1931.

96. When do we celebrate Independence Day?

Answer: July 4th.

Explanation: Independence Day, often known as the Fourth of July, commemorates the day in 1776 when the Declaration of Independence was adopted by the Continental Congress, marking the 13 colonies' official declaration of independence from Great Britain.

97. Name two national U.S. holidays.

Answer: New Year's Day and Independence Day (Other answers include Martin Luther King, Jr. Day, Presidents' Day, Memorial Day, Labor Day, Columbus Day, Veterans Day, Thanksgiving Day, and Christmas Day.)

Explanation: The U.S. celebrates various national holidays in honor of significant events, historical figures, and cultural practices. For instance, Independence Day celebrates the nation's declaration of independence, while New Year's Day marks the beginning of the calendar year.

98. Who was the first President of the United States?

Answer: George Washington.

Explanation: George Washington, often referred to as the "Father of His Country," was unanimously elected as the first President of the United States in 1789. He served two terms in office and set numerous precedents for the role and powers of the presidency.

99. Who is the "Father of Our Country"?

Answer: George Washington.

Explanation: George Washington is often referred to as the "Father of Our Country" because of the pivotal role he played in the founding of the United States. Not only was he the first President, but he also led the Continental Army to victory over the British during the Revolutionary War.

100. Who wrote the Declaration of Independence?

Answer: Thomas Jefferson.

Explanation: Thomas Jefferson, the third President of the United States, is credited with writing the initial draft of the Declaration of Independence in 1776. The document proclaimed the thirteen American colonies' independence from Great Britain and expressed the philosophical foundations of American democracy.

CHAPTER 7: AMERICAN HISTORY -A DEEP DIVE

America's rich tapestry is woven with the threads of determination, resilience, and a perpetual desire for freedom. As you embark on this journey to become a U.S. citizen, it's crucial to understand the historical milestones that shaped this great nation. This chapter endeavors to delve deeper into the pivotal events and figures that have forged the United States' unique identity. By understanding these roots, you not only prepare for the USCIS Civics Test but also develop a profound appreciation for your future homeland.

THE DAWN OF AMERICA: INDIGENOUS CIVILIZATIONS AND EARLY EXPLORERS

Before the arrival of European explorers, diverse Indigenous civilizations thrived across the continent. From the intricate societies of the Mississippian culture to the expansive trade networks of the Iroquois Confederacy, America's history started long before 1492. The understanding of this pre-colonial era is vital as it sets the stage for the subsequent periods of exploration and colonization.

1. The First Inhabitants: Indigenous Civilizations

- **The Mississippian Culture:** Centered around present-day Illinois, this civilization was distinguished by its vast city of Cahokia, which at its peak might have boasted a population larger than contemporary London. Known for their vast earthen mounds, the Mississippians had a complex societal structure and vast trade networks.

- **The Puebloans:** In the arid southwest, the Puebloans ingeniously engineered multi-storied cliff dwellings and cultivated the land using intricate irrigation systems. The spiritual core of their culture manifested in kivas, ceremonial pits used for rituals.

- **The Iroquois Confederacy:** In the northeastern woodlands, the Iroquois established a sophisticated democratic system, uniting five (later six) nations under a Great Law of Peace. Their confederacy, a shining testament to diplomacy and governance, influenced the crafting of the U.S. Constitution.

- **Nomadic Plains Tribes:** Roaming the vast plains were tribes like the Sioux and Cheyenne. Their cultures revolved around the buffalo, using it for food, clothing, and tools. With the introduction of the horse by Spanish settlers, they transformed into formidable equestrian societies.

2. A New Horizon: The European Explorers

The late 15th and early 16th centuries saw a flurry of European exploration. Driven by the allure of new trade routes and the quest for gold, explorers like Christopher Columbus set forth on treacherous voyages, culminating in the 'discovery' of the New World. While these explorations brought about increased interaction and eventually the colonization of the Americas, they also led to the decline of many Indigenous civilizations, mainly due to diseases and conflicts.

- **Christopher Columbus:** Sponsored by Spain in 1492, Columbus sought a direct route to Asia but instead stumbled upon the Bahamas in the Caribbean. Though he believed he'd reached the Indies, Columbus had ignited a European interest in a New World.

- **John Cabot:** Venturing from England in 1497, Cabot explored the northeastern part of North America, establishing an English claim to the continent.

- **Juan Ponce de León:** In 1513, this Spanish explorer arrived in what's now Florida, searching for the mythical Fountain of Youth. While he didn't find the fountain, he established the oldest European settlement in Puerto Rico and charted the Atlantic coastline.

- **Jacques Cartier:** Sailing for France, Cartier journeyed through the Gulf of St. Lawrence and up the St. Lawrence River in the 1530s, laying the groundwork for the French claim to Canada.

- **Hernán Cortés:** With a mix of military might and alliances with indigenous tribes, Cortés conquered the powerful Aztec Empire in Mexico by 1521, marking the beginning of Spain's vast empire in the Americas.

COLONIAL ERA: THE FOUNDATION STONES

The Colonial Era, spanning from the late 16th century to the late 18th century, was a transformative period that set the foundational stones for the United States. It's during these pivotal years that European powers, driven by ambitions of wealth, trade, and the propagation of their faiths, established colonies that would eventually come together to form a new nation. The stories of these colonies, their interactions with indigenous populations, and their internal dynamics, provide crucial insights into the early history of the U.S.

1. The Spanish in the South

Spain, buoyed by the early explorations of Columbus and others, became the first European power to establish colonies in the Americas. St. Augustine, founded in 1565 in present-day Florida, is the oldest European-established settlement within the U.S. borders.

The Spanish focused their efforts on converting indigenous people to Christianity and mining the region for precious metals. Their missions extended throughout the American Southwest and California.

2. English Establishments on the East Coast

Jamestown, Virginia: Founded in 1607, Jamestown was the first permanent English colony. Though faced with hardships like disease, conflicts with natives, and food shortages, the settlement persisted, especially after the introduction of tobacco cultivation.

Plymouth and Massachusetts Bay: Pilgrims seeking religious freedom established Plymouth in 1620. Later, the Puritans, also seeking religious refuge, founded Massachusetts Bay Colony. These colonies laid the roots of New England and were characterized by strong community ties and rigorous religious observance.

3. The Dutch and New Netherland

The Dutch, driven by their global trade ambitions, established New Netherland in 1624, which spanned parts of modern-day New York, New Jersey, Delaware, and Connecticut. The city of New Amsterdam, located on Manhattan Island, became a bustling trade center but was eventually seized by the English in 1664 and renamed New York.

4. Maryland and Pennsylvania: Havens of Religious Freedom

Maryland was established in 1632 as a refuge for English Catholics. However, it soon became home to various religious groups due to its policy of religious tolerance.

Pennsylvania, founded by William Penn in 1682, was a haven for Quakers and championed the ideals of religious freedom and pacifism.

5. Carolina, Georgia, and the Southern Colonies

The Carolinas (later split into North and South) were established in the late 1660s and became centers for tobacco and rice cultivation. Georgia, the last of the original thirteen colonies, was founded in 1732 as a buffer against Spanish Florida and as a place for England's indebted to start anew.

6. Interaction with Indigenous Populations

The arrival of European settlers drastically altered the lives of indigenous tribes. While there were moments of cooperation and mutual exchange, tensions frequently arose over land, resources, and cultural differences. These tensions often culminated in violent conflicts, leading to significant loss and displacement for indigenous communities.

7. The Tapestry of Colonial Life

Colonial life was a mosaic of cultures, beliefs, and lifestyles. While the colonists navigated challenges such as unfamiliar terrains and climates, they also forged dynamic communities, instituted governance structures, and laid the economic foundations of their settlements.

ROAD TO INDEPENDENCE

The road to American independence was not a sudden or impulsive journey. It was an evolutionary process, shaped by economic, social, political, and philosophical disagreements between the colonies and their British overlords. By delving into this

critical period, one gains a deeper understanding of the roots of American democracy and the sacrifices made to ensure its existence.

1. The Seeds of Discontent

Long before shots were fired, discontent was brewing. Colonists, especially in New England, had enjoyed a degree of autonomy thanks to Britain's policy of salutary neglect. However, the costly Seven Years' War (1754-1763) with France changed the dynamic. In a bid to recoup wartime expenses and tighten control over its colonies, Britain began imposing a series of taxes.

2. "Taxation Without Representation"

This slogan became the rallying cry against the British taxes. The Stamp Act (1765), which mandated tax stamps on printed materials, was the first to face significant opposition. This was followed by the Townshend Acts (1767), levying duties on numerous goods. Colonists viewed these acts as violations of their rights as English subjects, particularly since they had no representation in the British Parliament.

3. Boston Massacre and Boston Tea Party

In 1770, tensions escalated when British troops opened fire on a crowd in Boston, killing five colonists in what became known as the Boston Massacre. The event intensified anti-British sentiments. Three years later, the Tea Act led to the famous Boston Tea Party (1773), where colonists, protesting the monopoly granted to the East India Company, dumped an entire shipment of tea into Boston Harbor.

4. The Intolerable Acts

In retaliation for the Boston Tea Party, Britain passed the Coercive Acts (1774), dubbed the "Intolerable Acts" by the colonists. These acts closed the Boston Harbor and placed Massachusetts under direct British military control.

5. First Continental Congress

In response to the Intolerable Acts, representatives from 12 of the 13 colonies convened the First Continental Congress in Philadelphia in 1774. They sought to draft a unified response to British actions, resulting in the adoption of the Continental Association, which called for a boycott of British goods.

6. The Outbreak of War

The first shots of the Revolutionary War were fired on April 19, 1775, in the towns of Lexington and Concord, Massachusetts. The "shot heard 'round the world" marked the beginning of a full-blown war for independence.

7. The Declaration of Independence

Drafted primarily by Thomas Jefferson and adopted on July 4, 1776, by the Second Continental Congress, the Declaration of Independence proclaimed the colonies' freedom from British rule, outlining their grievances against King George III. It also put forth a philosophy of universal rights and the idea that government should be based on the consent of the governed.

8. The Revolutionary War

The war raged for eight years, with key battles such as Saratoga (1777) and Yorktown (1781) proving pivotal. Though facing a formidable enemy, the resilience, strategy, and foreign aid (especially from France) led the colonies to victory.

9. Treaty of Paris

In 1783, the Treaty of Paris was signed, formally ending the Revolutionary War and recognizing the United States of America's independence.

FORMING A NATION: TRIALS AND TRIUMPHS

The United States, after gaining independence, found itself on a challenging path. The newly freed nation faced the immense task of building its institutions, laws, and identity, all while navigating internal and external pressures. This era, defined by trial and error, ultimately shaped the pillars of American democracy.

1. The Articles of Confederation: A Weak Start

Before the Constitution, there was the Articles of Confederation, adopted in 1777. Serving as America's first constitution, it reflected the colonies' fear of a strong central authority. While it did provide for a united front during the Revolutionary War, its limitations became evident post-war. It lacked a central executive, had no power to tax, and couldn't regulate commerce.

2. Economic Challenges

Without the power to tax or regulate commerce, the new nation faced economic instability. States issued their own currencies, leading to inflation. Foreign trade suffered without a centralized negotiation authority. Additionally, war debts mounted, and the inability of the Confederation Congress to impose taxes meant states shouldered their own debts.

3. Shays' Rebellion: A Wake-Up Call

In 1786, Daniel Shays, a former war captain, led an uprising in Massachusetts protesting economic injustices, oppressive tax, and debt policies. Though the rebellion was quelled, it underscored the need for a stronger central government that could maintain order and ensure justice.

4. The Constitutional Convention of 1787

Recognizing the Articles' inefficacies, delegates from 12 states convened in Philadelphia. Initially meant to revise the Articles, the Convention soon embarked on drafting an entirely new constitution. Debates raged, particularly between small and large states and on the issue of slavery.

5. The Great Compromise

The Convention faced a deadlock over representation in the new Congress. Larger states favored representation based on population, while smaller states sought equal representation. The Connecticut Compromise, or the Great Compromise, proposed a bicameral legislature – the Senate with equal representation and the House of Representatives based on population.

6. Addressing Slavery

Slavery, a contentious issue, saw Southern states pushing for slaves to be counted for representation but not taxation. This led to the Three-Fifths Compromise, where three out of every five slaves would be counted for both tax purposes and representation.

7. Ratification and The Federalist Papers

For the Constitution to become law, nine out of thirteen states had to ratify it. This triggered intense nationwide debates between Federalists, who supported the

Constitution, and Anti-Federalists, who feared it centralized too much power. To champion ratification, Alexander Hamilton, James Madison, and John Jay penned The Federalist Papers, a series of essays explaining and defending the Constitution's provisions.

8. The Bill of Rights

By 1789, the Constitution was ratified, but there were still calls for better protection of individual rights. This led to the adoption of the first ten amendments, known as the Bill of Rights, in 1791. These amendments safeguarded fundamental freedoms like speech, religion, and assembly.

9. Building the Framework

With a ratified Constitution, the nation began building its framework. George Washington was inaugurated as the first President, establishing precedents for the office. The Judiciary Act of 1789 set up the federal judiciary, and the nation's capital was moved to its present location, Washington D.C..

20TH CENTURY: GLOBAL WARS AND CIVIL RIGHTS

The 20th century was an era of stark contrasts for America; it experienced the heights of economic prosperity and the depths of the Great Depression. It led in global conflicts for democracy and simultaneously wrestled with issues of civil rights and equality at home. This century forged the United States as a global superpower, both militarily and economically, while also forcing it to face its internal contradictions head-on.

1. World War I: The War to End All Wars

Entering late into the First World War in 1917, the U.S. played a crucial role in tipping the scales in favor of the Allies. The war profoundly impacted the nation, ushering in the Roaring Twenties, an era of prosperity and cultural dynamism.

2. The Roaring Twenties

A time of jazz, flappers, and a booming economy, the 1920s saw great technological and cultural shifts. Innovations like the automobile and radio reshaped everyday life, while the Harlem Renaissance celebrated African American culture and arts.

3. The Great Depression

The stock market crash of 1929 plunged the country into its most severe economic downturn. Millions lost jobs, faced evictions, and endured extreme poverty. This era reshaped the role of government in the economy, paving the way for Franklin D. Roosevelt's New Deal programs.

4. World War II: A Global Struggle

The attack on Pearl Harbor in 1941 propelled the U.S. into a global conflict. It played a pivotal role on multiple fronts, leading to eventual victories in both Europe and the Pacific. The war also accelerated the civil rights movement as African Americans, Latinos, and women took on critical roles in the workforce and military.

5. Cold War Tensions

Post-WWII, the U.S. and the Soviet Union emerged as superpowers, leading to the Cold War—a prolonged period of political tension, nuclear arms race, and proxy wars. It defined foreign policy, culminating in events like the Korean War, Cuban Missile Crisis, and the Vietnam War.

6. The Civil Rights Movement

The struggle for equality gained momentum in the 20th century. Leaders like Martin Luther King Jr. championed non-violent protests. Milestones included the Brown v. Board of Education ruling, the Civil Rights Act of 1964, and the Voting Rights Act of 1965, which sought to dismantle institutional racism.

7. Social Revolutions of the '60s and '70s

Alongside civil rights, the 1960s and '70s saw feminist movements, LGBTQ+ rights advocacy, and anti-war protests. The era was marked by significant shifts in societal norms, values, and the push for greater inclusivity and peace.

8. The Space Race

In competition with the USSR, the U.S. embarked on space exploration. This culminated in the Apollo 11 mission of 1969 when Neil Armstrong and Buzz Aldrin became the first humans to walk on the moon.

9. The Digital Revolution and the End of the Century

The late 20th century saw rapid technological advancements. The invention of the microprocessor, the rise of personal computers, and the birth of the internet set the stage for a digitally connected world in the years to come.

.

CHAPTER 8: THE STRUCTURE OF THE U.S. GOVERNMENT

Comprehending the elaborate structure of the U.S. federal government is critical for both the USCIS Civics Test and for anybody desiring be an active, educated person. The United States, with its distinct system of balances and checks, has actually laid the structure for modern-day democratic governance. This chapter will take you through the labyrinthine passages of the 3 branches of the U.S. federal government, clarifying their functions and significance.

1. THE LEGISLATIVE BRANCH: CRAFTING LAWS FOR THE NATION

The extremely heartbeat of a democratic country depends on its capability to make, change, and repeal laws that show the progressing requirements of its residents. At the core of this procedure in the United States is the Legislative Branch, a testimony to the vision of the nation's Founding Fathers.

1. Structure and Composition

The Bicameral System: The U.S. Congress, the legal body, is bicameral, including 2 homes-- the Senate and your house of Representatives.

The Senate: Comprising 100 members, 2 from each state, Senators serve six-year terms, with one-third of them up for reelection every 2 years.

The House of Representatives: With its subscription based upon state population, there are 435 Representatives. They serve two-year terms, making the whole House up for reelection every 2 years.

2. Key Powers and Duties

-Law-making: The main duty is the development of federal legislation. A costs can begin in either home, however both should concur for it to end up being law.

- Budget and Finance: Congress holds the handbag strings, licensing expenses by the federal government and raising nationwide profits.

- Oversight: Through different committees, Congress evaluations and monitors federal companies and programs, guaranteeing they run as meant.

- Impeachment: The House can impeach federal authorities, consisting of the President, with the Senate then holding the trial.

- Advise and Consent: The Senate contributes in authorizing governmental visits and validating treaties.

3. The Committee System

Varied in their functions, committees are where much of Congress's work is done. From the preliminary preparing to the refining of expenses, these smaller sized groups permit competence and concentrated on myriad topics.

4. The Process of Law-making

Beginning as a simple concept or proposition, costs go through strenuous analysis and adjustment. After committee assessments, disputes, and votes in both homes, just the most durable of costs reach the President's desk to be signed into law

5. Balancing Act: Representing Diverse Interests

With members from all corners of the nation, Congress embodies a myriad of top priorities and viewpoints. Stabilizing regional requirements with nationwide interests is a continuous obstacle..

6. Interactions with Other Branches

A system of balances and checks guarantees collective governance. While Congress makes laws, the Executive implements them, and the Judiciary translates them. The impact is shared: Congress can bypass governmental vetoes, authorize visits, and even form the judiciary's structure.

7. Challenges and Criticisms

The Legislative Branch, while effective, deals with obstacles. Partisanship, legal gridlock, and issues about representation and impact are regular topics of argument and criticism.

8. The Pulse of Democracy

Regardless of difficulties, the Legislative Branch stays important. It's a location where voices-- from the quietest to the loudest-- can affect the instructions of the country. Whether through the election of agents, open committee hearings, or public disputes, it's where the will of individuals discovers its most extensive expression

2. THE EXECUTIVE BRANCH: LEADING AND ENFORCING

The Executive Branch stands at the heart of the U.S. federal system, with its core objective being the enforcement of the country's laws. It runs as the face of the federal government both locally and worldwide, wielding significant impact and obligation.

1. Structure and Composition

- - The President: The U.S. President is both the president and the head of federal government. Chosen every 4 years, with the possibility of serving 2 terms, the President is accountable for maintaining the Constitution and guaranteeing that federal laws are consistently carried out.

- The Vice President: Serving as the second-highest authorities in the Executive Branch, the Vice President not just presumes governmental tasks if needed however likewise plays a critical function in the Senate, casting tie-breaking votes.

- The Cabinet: Comprised of the Vice President and the heads of 15 executive departments, the Cabinet supplies the President with suggestions and assists perform policy choices. These departments vary from the Department of State to the Department of Defense and more.

- Independent Agencies: Beyond the Cabinet departments are many independent companies and commissions, like NASA and the EPA, that meet specialized functions in the federal government..

2. Powers and Responsibilities

- Enforcement of Laws: The President makes sure that federal laws, gone by Congress, are carried out and implemented throughout the nation.

- Foreign Policy: The Executive Branch leads the country's diplomacy efforts, working out treaties, acknowledging foreign federal governments, and, with the correct permissions, releasing military forces.

- Veto Power: While Congress makes laws, the President has the power to ban them. Congress can bypass a veto with a two-thirds bulk in both homes.

- Executive Orders: These are regulations provided by the President that handle operations of the federal government. They bring the force of law, however can be withdrawn by subsequent presidents.

- Pardons and Reprieves: The President can give pardons or reprieves for federal criminal offenses, showcasing the branch's function in the justice system

3. Balances and Checks

To guarantee no branch ends up being too effective, the of the Constitution set up a system of balances and checks. The Executive Branch, for instance, can be inspected by the Judiciary (through judicial evaluation) and by Congress (through its financing power, impeachment procedures, and law-making capabilities).

4. The Executive in Times of Crisis

Throughout history, the function of the Executive Branch has actually broadened, specifically throughout crises. Whether it's Lincoln throughout the Civil War, FDR throughout the Great Depression, or modern-day obstacles, the Executive typically takes a leading edge in directing the country through hardship.

5. Criticisms and Challenges

The Executive Branch is not without its criticisms. Issues about "royal presidencies", prospective overreach, openness, and the balance in between nationwide security and specific rights have actually been frequent styles in American discourse.

6. The Heartbeat of Governance

It browses the nation through both chances and difficulties, constantly progressing, constantly at the pulse of the country's future and present..

3. THE JUDICIAL BRANCH: GUARDIANS OF THE CONSTITUTION

The Judicial Branch, among the 3 pillars of the U.S. federal government, plays an essential function in the country's constitutional system. It acts as the guardian of the Constitution, guaranteeing that the laws and actions of the land abide by the concepts preserved in this fundamental file.

1. Structure and Composition

The Supreme Court: At the helm of the Judicial Branch is the U.S. Supreme Court, consisted of 9 justices: one Chief Justice and 8 Associate Justices. Chosen by the President and verified by the Senate, these justices hold their positions for life, guaranteeing they make choices devoid of political pressures.

Federal Courts: Below the Supreme Court are the federal appellate courts, or Circuit Courts, and the federal district courts. These courts deal with cases including federal laws, conflicts in between states, and other particular locations set out in the Constitution.

2. Role and Functions

Judicial Review: One of the vital functions of the Judicial Branch is judicial evaluation-- the capability to take a look at federal and state laws and executive actions for their constitutionality. This power, though not clearly discussed in the Constitution, was developed in the landmark case of Marbury v. Madison in 1803.

Analysis of Laws: Courts play an important function in translating the significance and application of laws gone by Congress. Their analyses direct how laws are carried out and comprehended.

Dispute Resolution: At its core, the judiciary fixes disagreements, whether in between entities, states, or people, making sure that justice is portioned based upon legal concepts.

3. Checks and Balances

The radiance of the American constitutional system depends on its balances and checks. While the judiciary has the power of evaluation, its choices can be inspected by constitutional modifications. Furthermore, Congress holds the bag strings and can affect the courts by changing financing.

4. Landmark Cases and Their Impact

Throughout the years, the U.S. Supreme Court has actually provided judgments that have exceptionally affected American society and governance:

Brown v. Board of Education (1954): This choice stated racial partition in public schools unconstitutional, marking a turning point in the civil liberties motion.

Roe v. Wade (1973): This judgment acknowledged a lady's right to make choices about her own body, consisting of the right to an abortion, under the right to personal privacy.

Obergefell v. Hodges (2015): This case extended the right to wed same-sex couples, verifying that marital relationship is an essential right under the Fourteenth Amendment

5. The Importance of an Independent Judiciary

The framers of the Constitution envisioned a judiciary that could operate independently of political whims. An independent judiciary ensures that the rights and liberties enshrined in the Constitution are preserved and protected, even when they might be unpopular or under threat.

6. Challenges and Criticisms

Like all organizations, the Judicial Branch deals with criticisms and difficulties. Problems like judicial advocacy vs. restraint, the capacity for political predisposition in visits, and disputes over originalism vs. living constitution analysis are at the leading edge of conversations about the judiciary's function.

CHAPTER 9: SOCIETAL VALUES AND THE AMERICAN ETHOS

America's foundation rests not only on its political and historical milestones but also on the deeply entrenched values, cultural norms, and traditions that weave the diverse tapestry of the nation. For those on the precipice of citizenship, understanding these societal underpinnings is as essential as knowing the nation's political history.

1. The Melting Pot Theory

Often referred to as a "melting pot," America prides itself on being a fusion of cultures, religions, and ethnicities. This philosophy, dating back to the country's inception, promotes unity in diversity. It suggests that while individuals come from varied backgrounds, they melt into one shared national identity, preserving their unique traditions while contributing to the collective American ethos.

2. Core American Values

- Individualism: The belief in the unique value of each individual, promoting self-reliance, independence, and personal freedom.
- Equality: Rooted in the Declaration of Independence, it is the belief that everyone has equal rights regardless of their background.
- Liberty: The freedom to pursue one's goals, dreams, and way of life without undue constraints, so long as it does not harm others.
- Democracy: A deeply held value that promotes participation in governance and the principle that the majority's decision should prevail.

3. American Holidays and Their Significance

- Independence Day (July 4th): Celebrates the nation's declaration of independence from British rule in 1776.

- Thanksgiving: Traditionally observed on the fourth Thursday of November, it's a day for expressing gratitude, often commemorated with family gatherings.
- Veterans Day (November 11th): Honors military veterans for their service.
- Memorial Day: A day to remember and honor those who died while serving in the U.S. military.
- Labor Day: Honors the American labor movement and the contributions workers have made to the nation.

4. Symbolisms in the American Context

The American Flag: With its 13 stripes and 50 stars, it symbolizes the original colonies and current states, respectively, standing as a beacon of liberty and justice.

The Bald Eagle: Representing strength and freedom, it's the national bird and emblem.

The Statue of Liberty: A gift from France, this iconic statue stands as a symbol of freedom and democracy, welcoming immigrants to America's shores.

5. Cultural Milestones

Events like the Civil Rights Movement, Women's Suffrage, and LGBTQ+ rights have shaped America's cultural landscape, reflecting its evolving ethos and its commitment to ensuring rights for all its citizens.

6. The Role of Arts and Entertainment

American movies, music, literature, and sports aren't just entertainment; they are reflections of societal values, changes, and aspirations over the decades. From the jazz age, the rebellious rock 'n' roll era, to modern-day hip-hop, arts encapsulate the spirit of the times.

7. The American Dream

Central to the American ethos is the belief in the "American Dream" – the idea that anyone, regardless of where they come from, can achieve success through hard work and determination. This dream has drawn millions to its shores, seeking better opportunities and a chance at a brighter future.

CHAPTER 10: PREPARING FOR THE USCIS INTERVIEW: PRACTICE

INTRODUCTION

The USCIS interview is, without a doubt, a pivotal moment in the naturalization journey. While paperwork and tests play their part, this face-to-face interaction determines not just your knowledge, but your readiness to join the American citizenry. The key is to not just focus on the factual, but to genuinely represent yourself, your motivations, and your commitment. Let's explore how best to approach this momentous event.

1. UNDERSTANDING THE INTERVIEW'S PURPOSE

The interview serves multiple purposes:

- Verification of Documents: The officer reviews your application (Form N-400) and any accompanying documents.
- English Proficiency Test: You'll be tested on your ability to read, write, and speak English.
- Civics Test: A series of questions on U.S. history and government will be posed, of which you need to answer at least six correctly out of ten.
- Assessing Your Moral Character: This is more nuanced. The officer gauges if you align with the nation's principles and if there are any reasons you should not be granted citizenship.

2. EFFECTIVE COMMUNICATION: MORE THAN JUST ANSWERS

Active Listening

Listen to each question carefully. Ensure you understand what's being asked before you answer. If unsure, politely request clarification.

Clarity and Brevity

Your answers should be clear, concise, and directly related to the question. Resist the urge to provide unnecessary details.

Honesty is the Best Policy

Always tell the truth. Even if you believe a truth might be detrimental, it's better than being caught in a lie, which could jeopardize your entire application.

3. ANTICIPATING POTENTIAL QUESTIONS

While the questions related to your application are straightforward, others can be more personal or abstract. Here are some potential questions and strategies for framing your response:

1. "Why did you decide to apply for U.S. citizenship?"

Strategy: Speak from the heart. Highlight personal, professional, or civic reasons, such as wanting to vote, reuniting with family, or contributing more fully to the community.

2. "Have there been any changes to the information on your N-400 application since you filed it?"

Strategy: Regularly review your N-400 application before the interview. If there have been any changes, be transparent about them. Preparation is key.

3. "How did you and your spouse meet?" (If applicable)

Strategy: Provide a concise yet genuine account of your relationship journey. It's essential to be consistent with any previous statements or applications.

4. "What does the First Amendment guarantee?"

Strategy: Understand the core principles of the Constitution. Instead of rote memorization, relate it to real-life examples or news that resonates with you.

5. "Have you ever been arrested or committed a crime?"

Strategy: Honesty is imperative. If you've had encounters with the law, explain the situation factually and emphasize any lessons learned or restitution made.

6. "How do you support yourself financially?"

Strategy: Provide a clear overview of your employment or other sources of income. Having recent pay stubs or an employment verification letter can be helpful.

7. "Who is your current U.S. representative?"

Strategy: Stay updated on your local and federal representatives. Utilize government websites or apps that provide this information based on your address.

8. "Have you ever been involved in a group that advocated harm to the U.S.?"

Strategy: Answer truthfully. The USCIS checks backgrounds thoroughly. If you have a complicated history, consider consulting an immigration attorney beforehand.

9. "What do you value most about the U.S. and its principles?"

Strategy: Reflect on personal experiences or observations that highlight the freedoms, opportunities, or values you've come to appreciate in the U.S.

10. "How have you participated in your local community?"

Strategy: Share instances where you volunteered, attended community events, or otherwise engaged in civic activities. This showcases your commitment to being an active U.S. citizen.

11. "Can you describe the last election you were aware of, even if you didn't vote?"

Strategy: Stay informed about local and national elections. Understand key issues, candidates, and the results, as it demonstrates an interest in the U.S. democratic process.

12. "Do you plan to live in the U.S. permanently after becoming a citizen?"

Strategy: Your response should reflect your commitment to the U.S. If you have foreseeable reasons to travel or live abroad for short durations, clarify that the U.S. will be your permanent home.

13. "Describe the process of how a bill becomes a law in the U.S."

Strategy: Familiarize yourself with the basics of the legislative process. Even a simplified understanding of the steps involved will show your awareness of the workings of the U.S. government.

14. "How do you feel about jury duty?"

Strategy: Recognize that jury duty is both a right and a responsibility of U.S. citizens. Expressing a willingness to participate can highlight your commitment to civic duties.

15. "Who wrote the Declaration of Independence?"

Strategy: Remember key figures and their contributions to American history. Associating significant events or documents with visual or mnemonic devices can help in retaining this information.

16. "Have you traveled outside of the U.S. since you filed your application?"

Strategy: Maintain an up-to-date record of any travel dates and locations. This ensures accuracy and transparency when discussing any trips taken during the application process.

17. "What is the role of the Supreme Court?"

Strategy: Understand the core functions of major government institutions. Relate their significance to landmark decisions or current events to deepen your comprehension.

18. "How do you plan to contribute to the U.S. once you become a citizen?"

Strategy: Reflect on your aspirations, whether they're related to work, community involvement, or other forms of civic engagement. This is an opportunity to express your eagerness to be an active and contributing citizen.

19. "Name two rights only U.S. citizens have?"

Strategy: Differentiating between the rights of citizens and non-citizens is crucial. Regularly review and understand the unique rights that come with U.S. citizenship.

20. "Have you ever failed to file a required tax return in the U.S.?"

Strategy: Be forthright in your response. If there were any lapses, be prepared to explain the circumstances and emphasize any rectifications made.

21. "How do you handle disagreements or disputes in your community or workplace?"

Strategy: This question evaluates your adaptability and commitment to peaceful coexistence. Share instances where you demonstrated understanding, mediation, or compromise.

22. "Which war did General Eisenhower command U.S. forces in?"

Strategy: Take time to learn about major U.S. historical events and significant figures. Relating these figures to their respective eras or contributions can make remembering easier.

23. "What are the three branches of government and why are they significant?"

Strategy: Understand the concept of the separation of powers. Familiarize yourself with the specific roles of each branch to demonstrate a clear grasp of the American system of checks and balances.

24. "Why do you want to become a U.S. citizen?"

Strategy: This is a personal question, so reflect on your individual motivations. Whether they stem from familial, economic, educational, or ideological reasons, your sincerity is essential.

25. "Name one responsibility that is only for United States citizens."

Strategy: Familiarity with the distinction between the rights of residents and the exclusive responsibilities of citizens is paramount. This question tests that distinction.

26. "How does the Constitution protect individual rights?"

Strategy: Read up on the Bill of Rights and landmark Supreme Court cases. This shows an understanding of the foundational elements of U.S. democratic principles.

27. "What is the significance of Martin Luther King, Jr. in American history?"

Strategy: Learn about key figures in American civil rights history. Recognize their contributions and the impact of their efforts on present-day society.

28. "Describe the last election you followed or participated in."

Strategy: Displaying an active interest in civic responsibilities, like voting, underscores your commitment to being an engaged citizen.

29. "Which amendment grants freedom of speech?"

Strategy: Familiarize yourself with the essential amendments. Associating them with real-life examples or current events can aid retention.

30. "Who is your state's current Governor?"

Strategy: Along with federal knowledge, be aware of your state's local political figures. This showcases a comprehensive understanding of governance at all levels.

31. "How does the electoral college work?"

Strategy: Grasp the basics of the U.S. presidential election process. This is a frequent topic of interest, and understanding it highlights a deep engagement with civic mechanisms.

32. "What's your perspective on the American Dream?"

Strategy: Reflect on what the American Dream means to you personally. This question evaluates your alignment with foundational U.S. ideals.

33. "Name two National U.S. holidays and their significance."

Strategy: Be acquainted with major U.S. holidays and their historical or cultural importance.

34. "If needed, would you be willing to serve in the U.S. military?"

Strategy: This question gauges commitment to potential national responsibilities. Answer truthfully, understanding the gravity of the query.

35. "What are the rights or freedoms granted by the First Amendment?"

Strategy: Prioritize understanding the initial ten amendments, as they form the Bill of Rights and are central to U.S. democratic principles.

36. "How would you handle situations where your cultural values clash with American societal norms?"

Strategy: This probes adaptability and commitment to social cohesion. Highlight instances of understanding, learning, and harmonizing differing views.

37. "What does 'E Pluribus Unum' mean, and why is it significant?"

Strategy: Be familiar with U.S. mottos, symbols, and their significance. Such knowledge exhibits an understanding of the nation's shared identity.

38. "Name two members of the current U.S. Supreme Court."

Strategy: Keeping abreast with current members of key governmental institutions showcases a real-time interest in the nation's governance.

39. "How does one propose amendments to the U.S. Constitution?"

Strategy: Comprehend the process of how the Constitution can evolve. This shows an appreciation for the document's living nature.

40. "What's the importance of the Emancipation Proclamation?"

Strategy: Dive into crucial moments in American history. Recognize their legacy and how they shape modern America.

41. "Why is the U.S. described as a 'melting pot'?"

Strategy: Reflect on the rich tapestry of cultures, traditions, and histories in the U.S. This question assesses an understanding of American diversity and unity.

42. "How do you view your responsibilities towards your local community after becoming a citizen?"

Strategy: Think about community involvement, local issues, and any potential efforts you aim to support or spearhead. This underscores an intention to be an active, community-focused citizen.

43. "What role do checks and balances play in the U.S. government?"

Strategy: Familiarize yourself with the division of power between the three branches of government. Demonstrating your understanding of this concept shows a clear comprehension of the U.S. democratic system's safeguards.

44. "Can you explain the significance of the Statue of Liberty?"

Strategy: Dive into its history, the ideals it represents, and its role as a symbol of freedom and immigration. Sharing personal sentiments about its significance can make your answer resonate more.

45. "How do you feel about the Pledge of Allegiance?"

Strategy: Understand the history and significance of the Pledge. When answering, consider both the symbolic importance to the nation and its personal significance to you.

46. "Name two rights in the Declaration of Independence."

Strategy: Familiarize yourself with foundational documents and their core principles. Remember key phrases and their implications for U.S. history and society.

47. "What is the role of the Federal Reserve?"

Strategy: Brush up on key U.S. institutions and their functions. While some may not be directly tied to civics, their understanding demonstrates a comprehensive view of how the country operates.

48. "How does the Bill of Rights protect the rights of the citizens?"

Strategy: Dive into each amendment in the Bill of Rights. Being able to relate its provisions to real-world scenarios can enhance your understanding and the interviewer's perception of your preparation.

49. "What are the two parts of the U.S. Congress?"

Strategy: Understand the bicameral structure of the U.S. legislature. Explain their respective roles and significance in law-making.

50. "What is your perspective on U.S. foreign policies?"

Strategy: While this might seem like a loaded question, it's crucial to be informed about recent major foreign policy decisions. Share your views with clarity and respect, keeping in mind the broader American ethos.

51. "Why is freedom of the press essential to a democracy?"

Strategy: Understand the broader implications of each freedom granted by the Constitution. Relate the freedom of the press to the practicalities of transparent governance and informed citizenry.

52. "How would you explain federalism?"

Strategy: Understand the division of powers between state governments and the federal government. Showcasing this understanding displays a deeper grasp of the U.S. governmental structure.

53. "Who wrote the Star-Spangled Banner and why is it significant?"

Strategy: Know the historical context in which the national anthem was written. Relate its significance to national identity and shared values.

54. "What are the key principles of the U.S. Constitution?"

Strategy: Familiarize yourself with the Preamble and the core tenets of the Constitution. Discuss them not just as historical artifacts but as living principles that guide the nation.

55. "How do U.S. Senators get elected?"

Strategy: Be clear on the electoral process for different government roles. Distinguish between the processes for the House, the Senate, and the Presidency.

56. "How would you contribute to American society after naturalization?"

Strategy: Reflect on your personal, professional, and civic goals. Highlight intentions that resonate with communal upliftment and positive social contributions.

57. "What does the judicial branch do?"

Strategy: Understand the separation of powers and the specific role of the judiciary in interpreting laws and ensuring justice.

58. "How do amendments to the Constitution get ratified?"

Strategy: Grasp the two-step process of proposal and ratification. Emphasize the deliberate challenge built into altering the nation's foundational document.

59. "What does 'We the People' signify in the Constitution?"

Strategy: Reflect on the Constitution's democratic underpinnings. Relate it to the idea of a government by, for, and of the people.

60. "Why are there term limits for the U.S. President but not for members of Congress?"

Strategy: Understand the historical and practical reasons for this distinction. Reflect on the balance of power and checks on authority.

61. "What are your views on the U.S. education system?"

Strategy: Research on current educational policies, strengths, and challenges. Frame your answer with constructive feedback and optimism, highlighting the system's global reputation and potential areas for improvement.

62. "How has the U.S. influenced your life even before your decision to naturalize?"

Strategy: Reflect on personal experiences, whether through cultural influences, policy, or direct interactions. This ties your life journey to broader American societal waves, underlining the personal-professional interplay in your decision to naturalize.

63. "How do you interpret the American Dream?"

Strategy: Understand the historical context of the term and its evolution over time. Reflect on your aspirations and how they align with the broader idea of opportunity and upward mobility in America.

64. "Who are the founding fathers and what is their significance?"

Strategy: Familiarize yourself with the key figures of the American Revolution and the early Republic. Understand their contributions and how their ideas shape contemporary American values.

65. "What role do political parties play in the U.S.?"

Strategy: Grasp the two-party system, its origins, and its function in U.S. elections and policy-making. Discuss with a neutral stance, showcasing an understanding rather than bias.

66. "How would you describe the civil rights movement?"

Strategy: Dive into the history, key figures, and milestones of the movement. Relate its significance to the broader themes of justice, equality, and American ideals.

67. "What are your thoughts on the U.S. healthcare system?"

Strategy: Research the current healthcare landscape, its strengths, and challenges. Answer diplomatically, balancing critique with recognition of its merits.

68. "How do state governments differ from the federal government?"

Strategy: Understand the division of powers in the U.S. system of federalism. Be able to elucidate the unique roles and responsibilities of state versus federal entities.

69. "Why is the U.S. referred to as a 'melting pot'?"

Strategy: Delve into the history of immigration and cultural assimilation in the U.S. Reflect on the nation's diverse fabric and the harmonious blend of cultures.

70. "What are the key responsibilities of a U.S. citizen?"

Strategy: Beyond just listing duties like voting or jury service, elaborate on the ideological responsibilities, such as upholding American values and contributing to community welfare.

71. "How is the U.S. judicial system structured?"

Strategy: Understand the hierarchical structure from local courts to the Supreme Court. Highlight the principles of justice, checks and balances, and the rule of law.

72. "What importance does the Second Amendment hold in contemporary America?"

Strategy: Familiarize yourself with the text, historical context, and current debates surrounding the Second Amendment. Approach this topic neutrally, showcasing an understanding of both its historical significance and modern implications.

73. "How do the mid-term elections work?"

Strategy: Understand the electoral cycle, the offices up for election during the mid-terms, and their significance in shaping the legislative landscape.

74. "Describe the process of impeaching a president."

Strategy: Grasp the constitutional provisions for impeachment, the roles of the House and Senate, and the historical instances of impeachment. Focus on the process rather than political implications.

75. "What are your views on the U.S. tax system?"

Strategy: Research the basics of the U.S. taxation system and recent reforms. Answer should balance understanding of its necessity with any critiques on its complexities or inequalities.

76. "How would you explain the concept of 'separation of powers'?"

Strategy: Dive into the division of responsibilities among the three branches of government. Elaborate on the importance of this principle in safeguarding democracy.

77. "Who is the Chief Justice of the United States, and why is their role vital?"

Strategy: Stay updated on the current Chief Justice and understand the significant duties of this role, especially in guiding the judicial branch and interpreting the Constitution.

78. "What does 'E Pluribus Unum' mean and why is it significant?"

Strategy: Translate and relate the motto to the country's history, emphasizing the unity and diversity inherent in the U.S.

79. "How are constitutional amendments proposed?"

Strategy: Understand the formal mechanisms for suggesting changes to the Constitution, including the role of Congress and state conventions.

80. "What is the significance of the Emancipation Proclamation?"

Strategy: Recognize its role in the Civil War, the broader fight against slavery, and its implications for civil rights in America.

81. "What principles guide U.S. foreign policy?"

Strategy: Familiarize with key tenets like democracy promotion, human rights, and national security. Highlight the balance of ideological goals with practical international considerations.

82. "How do you interpret the First Amendment and its protections?"

Strategy: Understand the range of freedoms it guarantees and their significance in maintaining a vibrant, democratic society.

83. "How do the three branches of government keep each other in check?"

Strategy: Familiarize yourself with the checks and balances system. Illustrate how each branch can limit or control the powers of the other two, ensuring no single branch becomes too powerful.

84. "Describe the Bill of Rights."

Strategy: Understand the initial ten amendments to the U.S. Constitution, their history, and their ongoing significance in safeguarding individual liberties against governmental overreach.

85. "What is the role of the Federal Reserve in the U.S. economy?"

Strategy: Grasp the basics of the Federal Reserve's duties, including its control over monetary policy, and its impact on interest rates and inflation.

86. "Why was the U.S. Constitution created?"

Strategy: Understand the failures of the Articles of Confederation and the desire for a stronger, unified government that still upheld individual freedoms.

87. "How do you view the significance of the Civil Rights Act of 1964?"

Strategy: Acknowledge its role in ending segregation in public places and employment discrimination. Discuss the broader impacts on society and subsequent movements for equality.

88. "What are your thoughts on the electoral college system?"

Strategy: Comprehend the mechanics of the electoral college and its historic foundations. Be ready to discuss its pros and cons in the context of democratic representation.

89. "Describe the U.S.'s role in the United Nations."

Strategy: Understand the U.S.'s role as one of the founding members and a permanent member of the Security Council. Be aware of the U.S.'s contributions and its stance on major global issues.

90. "What is the 19th Amendment and why is it significant?"

Strategy: Recognize its role in granting women the right to vote, and its importance in the broader context of women's rights and equality movements.

91. "How does the U.S. Census impact political representation?"

Strategy: Understand the decennial census's role in reapportioning the House of Representatives and redrawing district boundaries, ensuring representation is in line with population shifts.

92. "What role does the Cabinet play in the U.S. government?"

Strategy: Familiarize yourself with the Cabinet's advisory role to the President and the heads of executive departments who comprise it. Know their role in policy-making and administration.

93. "Why is freedom of the press vital to a democracy?"

Strategy: Reflect on the press's role in informing the public, holding power accountable, and upholding democratic ideals of transparency and openness.

94. "What's the difference between the House of Representatives and the Senate?"

Strategy: Understand the different responsibilities, term lengths, and representation criteria (population vs. equal per state) of the two chambers of Congress.

95. "How does the impeachment process differ for federal judges compared to the president?"

Strategy: While the House of Representatives still initiates the process, know the differences in reasons for impeachment and the historical context behind each.

96. "Describe the importance of the Declaration of Independence."

Strategy: Reflect on its historic significance in declaring U.S. independence and its broader philosophical foundations for the new nation's ideals.

97. "How is the U.S. military structured?"

Strategy: Familiarize yourself with the various branches of the military, their roles, and their command hierarchy.

98. "What are the primary objectives of U.S. domestic policy?"

Strategy: Understand the broad goals of domestic policy, from ensuring economic stability to promoting individual welfare and civil rights.

99. "What is the role of the Supreme Court in the U.S. judicial system?"

Strategy: Comprehend the Court's role in interpreting the Constitution, its power of judicial review, and its impact on American laws and society.

100. "How do primary elections function in the U.S.?"

Strategy: Understand the purpose of primaries in selecting party candidates for general elections, the difference between open and closed primaries, and their role in shaping political landscapes.

101. "What do you know about the American involvement in World War II?"

Strategy: Grasp the U.S.'s transition from neutrality to active involvement, key battles, and the broader implications of the war for American society and global position.

102. "How do local governments function in the U.S.?"

Strategy: Understand the roles and responsibilities of city councils, mayors, and other local entities in governing and making decisions at the community level.

5. FINAL TIPS FOR THE DAY

Stay Calm and Composed: It's natural to feel nervous but try to channel that energy positively. Deep breaths, meditation, or even a brisk walk can help clear your mind and reduce anxiety.

Rest and Refresh: A good night's sleep can work wonders. Ensure you get adequate rest the night before so you're alert and attentive.

Dress Appropriately: While there's no strict dress code, opt for business-casual attire. This not only boosts your confidence but also conveys respect for the process.

Documentation Ready: Organize all the necessary documents the night before. Make sure you have originals and copies, as needed.

Early Arrival: Aim to arrive at least 15-30 minutes before your scheduled time. This will give you a buffer in case of unexpected delays and also allow you a moment to gather your thoughts.

Practice Active Listening: Focus on understanding the interviewer's questions thoroughly before you respond. If you didn't understand, it's okay to politely ask them to repeat or clarify.

Honesty is the Best Policy: If you're unsure about an answer, it's better to admit it than to fabricate a response. The interviewers value honesty.

Engage in Mock Interviews: If possible, practice with friends or family. This helps familiarize you with potential questions and hones your responses.

Stay Updated: While you've been preparing for a while, it's beneficial to skim through current events or any recent changes in policies just before the day.

Positive Mindset: Visualize a successful interview outcome. Believe in your preparation, and remember why you embarked on this journey to begin with.

Seek Support: Talk to others who have gone through the process, join support groups, or engage in community events. Sharing experiences and garnering insights can be immensely helpful.

Reflect on Your Journey: Take a moment to acknowledge how far you've come. This isn't just about facts or figures but understanding and connecting deeply with the essence of becoming an American.

CHAPTER 11: LANGUAGE PROFICIENCY – MORE THAN JUST SPEAKING

THE SIGNIFICANCE OF ENGLISH PROFICIENCY

The journey towards U.S. citizenship is not just about understanding the nation's history or its political framework. A key component of this journey is mastering the English language – in reading, writing, and speaking. The United States Citizenship and Immigration Services (USCIS) places a high premium on language proficiency, seeing it as essential for an individual's integration and active participation in American civic life.

THE THREE PILLARS: READING, WRITING, AND SPEAKING

Reading: This skill is crucial for everyday tasks like understanding news, following written instructions, or comprehending official documents. On the citizenship test, you'll be provided sentences to read aloud. Your comprehension and pronunciation will be assessed.

Tip: Diversify your reading materials. Start with children's books or simple news articles and progressively move to more complex materials. Highlight words you don't understand and use dictionaries or apps to understand and remember them.

Writing: Being able to convey thoughts clearly in written form is vital. During the test, you'll be asked to write a sentence dictated to you, testing your grammar and spelling.

Tip: Practice writing daily. Start with simple sentences about your day, and gradually move to more intricate topics. Use tools like Grammarly to check for errors and improve.

Speaking: This is the most interactive aspect of the test. The entire interview process tests your speaking skills, from answering questions about your application to discussing American civics.

Tip: Engage in English conversations regularly. Language exchange meetups, English classes, or even practicing with a fluent friend can be beneficial.

STRATEGIES TO IMPROVE PROFICIENCY

1. Immersive Learning

Watch English Television and Movies: Use subtitles initially, then try to watch without them to test comprehension. Over time, movies and TV shows will expose you to different accents, slangs, and cultural nuances.

Listen to English Music or Podcasts: The rhythm and melodies of songs can help memorize new vocabulary, while podcasts on topics of interest can improve listening skills.

Read Out Loud: Whether it's a book, a news article, or a grocery list, reading out loud can improve pronunciation and fluency.

2. Daily Practice

Keep a Diary: Writing a few lines about your day can help in structuring your thoughts in English and enhance writing skills.

Set Aside Dedicated Time: Even 15 minutes of daily focused practice can make a difference over time.

Engage in Conversations: Speak with native speakers or fellow learners. Regular interaction is key to enhancing speaking skills.

3. Leverage Technology

Use Language Learning Apps: Platforms like Duolingo, Babbel, or Rosetta Stone offer interactive exercises that cater to different learning styles.

Watch YouTube Tutorials: Many educators provide free lessons, ranging from basic grammar to advanced conversation techniques.

Join Online Language Exchanges: Websites like Tandem or HelloTalk allow you to connect with native speakers keen on learning your language. This mutual exchange can be incredibly beneficial.

4. Join Formal Classes

Enroll in ESL Classes: Many community colleges, universities, and community centers offer English as a Second Language (ESL) courses.

Hire a Tutor: A personal tutor can provide one-on-one sessions tailored to your specific needs and pace.

5. Engage in Group Activities

Book Clubs: Joining or forming an English book club can improve reading skills and offer a platform for discussions.

Discussion Groups: Be it current affairs, movies, or culture – discussing various topics can widen vocabulary and improve articulation.

Participate in Public Speaking Clubs: Organizations like Toastmasters offer a structured environment to improve public speaking and leadership skills in English.

6. Travel or Live in an English-speaking Environment

Short Stays: Even a brief vacation in an English-speaking country can expose you to the language in a real-world context.

Prolonged Stays: If possible, consider studying or working in an English-speaking country. Continuous exposure is one of the best ways to attain fluency.

7. Consistent Feedback

Ask for Corrections: When practicing, request friends, teachers, or peers to correct your mistakes.

Record Yourself: Listening to your own pronunciation can highlight areas for improvement.

8. Vocabulary Building

Flashcards: A classic but effective method. Write the English word on one side and its meaning or translation on the other.

Word-a-Day Challenge: Learn and use a new word every day.

9. Grammar Focus

Workbooks: Invest in a good English grammar workbook. Regular exercises can firm up understanding.

Online Grammar Checkers: Tools like Grammarly can be integrated into daily life to improve writing skills.

10. Stay Motivated and Patient

Remember that language learning is a marathon, not a sprint. Celebrate small milestones and remember why you started this journey. With determination and the right strategies, achieving proficiency is not just a possibility but a guarantee.

Overcoming Challenges

Language learning can be challenging, and it's natural to feel overwhelmed or discouraged at times. Remember, everyone progresses at their own pace. Celebrate small victories, whether it's learning a new word or successfully holding a conversation.

Why Proficiency Matters

Language is more than just a means of communication. It's a bridge to understanding a culture, its nuances, and its people. By striving to achieve English proficiency, you're not only preparing for a test but also equipping yourself to be an active, informed, and integrated member of the American community.

CHAPTER 12: THE ENGLISH TEST - STRATEGIES FOR SUCCESS

In the path to U.S. citizenship, the English test is an essential milestone that gauges an applicant's proficiency in the English language. It is divided into three core components: reading comprehension, writing, and speaking. While many might be daunted by the thought of this exam, the right preparation strategies can simplify the process and lead to success. This chapter will delve into each component and offer techniques and insights to help you excel.

1. READING COMPREHENSION

Reading comprehension not only tests your ability to understand words but also to grasp the context and meaning behind sentences and paragraphs.

- Skimming Technique: Before diving deep into the content, skim through it quickly to get an overall sense. This gives a general idea and can guide you on what to expect.

- Highlighting Key Points: While practicing, underline or highlight main ideas or unfamiliar words. This habit can improve focus and retention.

- Practice with Varied Materials: Don't just limit yourself to test samples. Read newspapers, magazines, and online articles to expose yourself to diverse language structures and vocabulary.

- Inference Skills: Some questions might require you to infer information that isn't directly stated. Practice this skill by trying to deduce unstated details in what you read.

2. EFFECTIVE WRITING

The writing portion evaluates your ability to convey ideas clearly and correctly.

- Structure is Key: Always start with a clear topic sentence followed by supporting details and a conclusion. This structure ensures clarity.

- Expand Your Vocabulary: While practicing, use a thesaurus to learn synonyms for commonly used words. This not only enhances your writing but also impresses the evaluator.

- Avoid Complex Sentences: While it's tempting to use intricate structures, simple sentences often convey ideas more clearly. Focus on clarity over complexity.

- Proofread: Always revisit what you've written to correct any grammatical or spelling mistakes.

3. CLEAR SPOKEN ENGLISH

The spoken component assesses your ability to understand and respond to questions in English.

- Listen Actively: Before responding, ensure you understand the question. If unsure, don't hesitate to ask the interviewer to repeat or clarify.

- Practice Pronunciation: Certain English sounds can be challenging. Use online resources to listen and practice these sounds.

- Engage in Conversations: The more you speak, the better you get. Engage in conversations with native speakers or join English speaking clubs.

- Think Aloud: When alone, think in English and speak your thoughts out loud. This habit can improve fluency and reduce the need to translate from your native language during the test.

CONCLUSION

As we close this comprehensive guide, it's essential to remember that the pursuit of American citizenship isn't just a personal journey—it's a testament to the diverse, enduring fabric of the United States. Every individual who undertakes this path strengthens the nation's character, adding unique stories, experiences, and values to its rich tapestry.

The naturalization process, as detailed throughout this guide, is rigorous and demands dedication. Yet, it is a reflection of the United States' commitment to ensuring its citizens appreciate and uphold the core principles upon which it was founded. By the time you've reached this point in your preparation, you have not only familiarized yourself with essential facts and procedures but also delved deep into the ethos and values that make America truly unique.

Remember, citizenship is not merely about rights—it's about responsibilities. As you stand on the threshold of becoming an American citizen, you're embracing a role that champions democracy, liberty, and the pursuit of happiness. This new chapter in your life offers not just personal opportunities but the chance to contribute positively to a nation that thrives on the collective dreams and aspirations of its people.

While this guide has equipped you with knowledge and strategies, your personal dedication, resilience, and commitment to the ideals of the U.S. are what will truly guide you through the final stages. Surround yourself with a supportive community, keep abreast of any policy changes, and always believe in the dream that brought you here.

In the words of former President Barack Obama, "America is not the project of any one person. The single-most powerful word in our democracy is the word 'We.' 'We

The People.' 'We Shall Overcome.' 'Yes, We Can.'" As you step into the role of an American citizen, remember that you are now an integral part of this 'We,' and together, there's nothing we can't achieve.

Thank you for allowing this guide to be a part of your journey, and congratulations on reaching this pivotal moment in your life. Embrace the challenges, cherish the privileges, and above all, believe in the power of your American Dream. Welcome to the beginning of your new chapter. Welcome home.

Gain secure access to our exclusive Bonuses download by simply scanning the QR code!

Made in the USA
Las Vegas, NV
06 November 2023

80337509R00059